MW01275740

OUT OF OREGON

Logging, Lies
and
Poetry

Michael J. Barker

ISBN: 0-9743148-0-3

Printed in the United States of America by
Maverick Publications • Bend, Oregon

Dedication

Stalwart ghosts of the tall deep woods,
'twas not blood, but pitch in their veins.
Memories wane of the mountain and her moods,
and history tells of the little that remains.
Like a harlot she beckoned you to her breast,
and like the fools you were you came.
The unworthy and weak she lay to rest,
right where they fell in a grave with no name.

This book is dedicated to those men (past and present)
who by their pluck, wrest their bounty from the good earth,
and do so in high spirits and of their own accord.
Their dogged determination, blatant courage,
and ingenuity lend an endearing legacy to the spirit
of this endangered species... 'The logger.'

Oh Stranger, ponder well, what breed of men were these
Cruisers, Fallers, Skinners, Ox, Horse, and 'Cat'
Choker setters and the rest who used these tools.
No summers searing dust could parch their soul,
Nor bitter breath of winter chill their hearts.
'Twas never said "they work for pay alone"
Tho it was good and always freely spent.
Tough jobs to lick they welcomed each day,
"We'll bury that old mill in logs," their boast,
such men as these have made this country great.
Beyond the grasp of smaller, meaner men.
Pray God, Oh Stranger, others yet be born
Worthy as they to wear a logger's boots.

"Ode to the Loggers"
By Nelson Reed

iii

Acknowledgments

The truth be known, I think all of the people who have helped me out on this project should get most of the credit. I literally could not have done it without them, that is the honest truth, as you will soon discover in reading this book, I am not a writer, hell, I didn't even gradiate from high school, or low school neither!

First on the list is my wife of 28 years, Kristine. She has put up with my gallivanting, gypo logger escapades longer than either of us cares to remember. She has weathered countless nights of elbow bending, beer swilling marathons, wondering if I would make it home in one piece, and probably sometimes wishing I wouldn't! She raised two fine young men, with the wolf right outside the door the whole damn time, and nursed me through the ups and downs that only a logger and his family can know, and with 15 surgeries to boot! I love you, sweetie.

Next, all of my rowdy loggin' pards, most of us are still around, some are not, and those before us who blazed the way and inspired us, this book is for you, boys.

There's Warnie Points and his wife Ardis, God rest her soul, how they put up with me and my buddy Woodrow through the rowdy years, and them two kids of ours, I'll never know. I'll never forget all they've done for us.

My youngest son, Eric, aka, "The Dropout," who did all of the artwork for the book, he no doubt has his father's artistic traits, and educational background!

Dale Crocker of Sweet Home, Oregon, who gave me my first logging job. Also his side rod, Dave Walker, who probably wanted to fire me a dozen times while I was learning the trade.

Dick Renoud and Gary Betz, also of Sweet Home, thanks for all the draws guys, I wrote a poem about it!

Mert, Marvin, and Mary Menge from Pleasant Hill; Mert is arguably one of the most talented chain saw artists around, you are a big part of the book guys.

Many thanks to Dr. Don and Carol Schroeder, of Eugene, owners of the Bison-Ten-Yal Ranch, and those magnificent animals they raise. Doc patched me up so many times we became friends, and when I became too busted up to log any longer, I was their ranch hand for over four years. It was by their actions that my first poem was published, and because of that, I became serious about poetry. I can't thank them enough.

When I decided to write Out of Oregon, I wanted to do it on the Rogue River, just like Zane Grey did: enter Court and Dawn Boice, owners of Paradise Lodge.

I worked for them for over a year and a half, and wrote most of my book, at Paradise; I did my first public recitals in front of the river rock fire place at the lodge, and became more confident each time, thank you both so very much.

And there's the Rogue River sheriff himself, Alan Boice, tough as they come, and my good friend to this day. There's Ernie Rutledge, owner of Illahee Lodge, he helped save my life by getting me out of there when I had pneumonia and a temperature of 106 degrees.

I can't leave out Mother Nature, aka Virginia Wierbinski of Agness, Oregon, my Rogue River sweetie, you are all very special people, and I'm a better person from knowing you, my best wishes to you all.

Finley Hays, founder of Loggers World, for his advice and encouragement, a logger's logger, from the old school. Thank you sir, for your advice and direction.

Mike Thoele, accomplished author and journalist, thanks for all of your help Mike.

Bobbie Kipp, and her husband Ron, respectively office manager and gardener at Paradise Lodge. They unselfishly gave of their time and hospitality to do the editing for me, and let me use their guest house on the banks of the Rogue, I am eternally grateful for all that you've done, what wonderful people you are.

Many thanks to Christina Cameron, who helped out with the final editing on such short notice, actually with no notice. Editing for me is, politely put, interesting, as all of the people who helped out on this project can attest. I can't thank you all enough.

And to my mentor, and in my opinion, the greatest poet to ever pen a verse, the Bard of the Yukon himself, Robert W. Service; truly a gifted poet. I've read and admired his way with verse since boyhood.

And last, but certainly not least, L. L. "Stub" Stewart. What can I say about this man that hasn't already been said a dozen times? A legend in his own time, timber baron, lumber and plywood magnate, retired army officer, combat veteran of WWII, politician, community leader, and philanthropist, who has given to his fellow man and community his whole life.

Aside from my marriage, and the birth of my two sons, the highlight of my life was to have Stub, his girlfriend Jane, John Blackwell, Former President of the World Forestry Center, and his wife, Christina up at the lodge for Stub's 92nd birthday, for three wonderful days. I was honored to recite my poetry for them each night, I will always treasure that special time.

Stub opened many doors for me in the production of this book, He set me up with Mike Thoele, and not once, but twice loaned me his personal copy of the book, "Bohemia; The Lives and Times of an Oregon Timber Venture", so wonderfully written by Mr. Thoele, so I could do the research for "The Ballad of Bohemia." I just hope I can do it the justice it is deserving of.

Out of the kindness of his heart Stub helped me finance this book, just to know that he would do that for me is worth more than selling a million copies of my book. My sincere and heartfelt thanks Stub, for all of your help and encouragement.

Foreword

Out of Oregon is a collection of poetry and short stories which pays tribute to a breed of men whose patience and courage played a big part of the shaping of our great nation from its infancy to the superpower it is today.

The legacy of those early loggers does indeed live on in today's "woods warriors". Granted, their labors today are far and above easier than those of their predecessors, due largely in part to a technological revolution that has mechanized the industry in ways unimaginable to those men of just a few short decades ago. The old adage, "the times, they are a changin'", holds true with the wood products industry, probably more so than with many other natural resource industries.

Long gone are the days of the cut and run mentality, which was so prevalent in those early days. The industry has been forced to come to grips with the fact that it does not have an endless supply of timber, as was once the popular opinion. It must strive to find that happy medium between its own survival and the conservation of the delicate environment from which sustains it.

Though this new generation of loggers has at its fingertips "new-fangled contraptions" that make ease of what was once back breaking labor, it is easy to see that the pride and camaraderie inherent to the loggers of old is still alive and well today. The work is still hard and dangerous, and men still die, just as they always have, and always will. The days still start in the wee hours and end in the evening with long commutes each way the norm, hence the saying: "two moonlight rides and a picnic lunch". It is still not a job for the weak or faint of heart.

The days of the logging camps have long since vanished. Along with them, the old narrow gauge rail lines that hauled logs to the mill with an old steam engine that chugged and clacked its way up and down the mountains, and over precarious looking trestles into the steam powered mills. Never again will we see 150' Douglas fir spar poles rigged with tons of blocks and cables stretching out thousands of feet across canyons to bring their treasure from the forests. No more will boys grease the plank roads, so the ox and bulls can inch their loads to a rail siding. Gone are sounds and smells of the old steam donkeys, and the stench of the bunkhouse, the old wigwam saw dust burners slowly rust away, but remain a solemn testimony to the demise of a way of life that is constantly on the ropes, taking blow after blow, but will never give up. Not as long as there are men worthy enough to claim the title of "logger", because not just anybody can be a logger, it takes men to fill those boots.

Table of Contents

SEPTEMBER ELEVENTH

We won't soon forget that September morning,
As we stared unbelieving at hell in the skies.
When cowards came calling without mercy or warning,
And left us dumbfounded with tears in our eyes.

Thick smoke and flames stole a beautiful blue sky,
As cold fear and raw panic manifest in us all.
Then the whole of creation looked up and cried, "why",
As those Twin Towers shuddered and started their fall.

The deadly confetti fluttered down in the breeze,
As those in the streets ran hard for their lives.
Even the tough guys felt weak in the knees,
As people world wide lost husbands and wives.

What sort of demons would conceive such a deed,
And have the gall, to do it in the name of our God?
May he pity the savages with such hatred to feed,
Martyrs to Satan like peas in the pod.

First blood is drawn the line has been crossed,
The fate of mankind laid out on the table.
This terror must end no matter the cost,
Keepers of the peace, be vigilant and able.

Lessons are taught, but too soon forgot,
Complacency rewards a life void of war.
The giants awoke for the battle to be fought,
Remember September, for now and evermore.

1

THE BOYS AND I

To be among the bison,
Is to go back to another time.
I've come to love the boys so much,
Sometimes I think they're mine.

I've fed them hay and tended them,
In driving wind and rains.
I've closed my eyes, seen millions of them,
Roaming on the plains.

I've heard them roar like lions,
And been among them on the prong.
I've seen them run all out,
They let me ride along.

I've had a one ton bull,
Twelve inches from my face.
I looked him in the eye,
And he put me in my place.

I've held a newborn calf,
Still wet, so red, and alert.
And I rubbed an old cow's nose,
While she lay dying in the dirt.

They don't know how to steal,
Or could never tell a lie.
It leaves me cold to see the herd,
Against the evening sky.

The town is closing in on us,
At a real steady pace.
I wish they'd all just up and leave,
'Cause the Boys, they need their space.

I hope that when my time has come,
And I've spoken my last word.
The good Lord would see it fit,
To leave me with the herd.

Bison Calf

Buffalo "Bill"

BISON RANCHIN'

In my early forties, it became clear that after all of my surgeries it was time to get out of the woods, while the getting was still good. Over the years I had became friends with my doctor, orthopedic surgeon, Donald J. Schroeder. Doc has an interesting hobby, he raises bison, and is the owner of The Bison Ten Yal Ranch.

I started out by my career in bison ranchin' feeding the herd for him while he and his wife Carol were out of town on doctoring business and vacations. At that time there were about 30 or 40 head that he ran on 130 some acres on Fir Butte Rd., on the outskirts of Eugene, Or. Being a logger, the only contact I'd ever had with a dad gum bison was by watching Dances With Wolves. Boy was I about to get an education.

After being around these creatures for a few years, it is easy to see why the Native Americans held them in such high esteem, and in fact worshiped them. The bison was their sustenance and livelihood, the very foundation of their society and was always treated with reverence and dignity. No animal was ever taken without a ceremony given and homage paid, as it should be.

When the white man came along and the Indian wars began, the plan of decimating the bison herds to starve out the Indians was undertaken. The result was a catastrophe of epic proportion, damn near resulting in the extinction of these hardy creatures. Pretty smart, huh? The number of animals remaining after the slaughter is open for debate, so for sake of argument we'll say 1,000. Some say more, some say less, it doesn't really matter. The number of animals before the massacre is also disputed, estimates range from 40 to 60 million, this is including Canada. It is estimated that the Indians harvested about 3 million animals a year.

Bison calves are born in the spring of the year after a gestation period of nine months. They are cute little buggers, reddish in color and weighing around 25 pounds, markedly smaller than their bovine cousins. Immediately after birth, the mother gets the little one on its feet, if

5

it needs help, most do not, and it goes to the tit immediately. If it does not nurse and get the colostrum it will die, there are no exceptions. It is the drink of life for them, it contains all the antibodies that are essential for the development of its immune system, and its survival.

These young ones can keep up with the herd one hour after birth and their mothers are fiercely protective of them, as is the rest of the herd. A healthy bull in the wild can grow to 2,000 pounds or more, be over 6 feet tall at the hump, measure over twelve feet in length, and gallop at 30 mph for half a day. Bison are not known for having a friendly disposition, every year someone is seriously injured or killed by one when they push the envelope.

Bison have what we call "the bubble". This is an area of about a six foot circle around the animal, if you crowd him and he feels threatened, you're dead. He will warn you by arching his tail up, resembling a hairy cobra, he will nod his head, paw the ground and let loose with a guttural roar similar to a lion. If one doesn't heed these warnings, it's adios amigos.

Mating season is often the time of some horrific battles between aspiring suitors. The very basis of all creatures survival, (with the exception of man) is survival of the fittest. In other words the winner of the fight gets the girls, all of them, although sometimes during a fight some lesser bulls have been known to sneak in and breed a cow or two while the battle is raging.

Bison are superb swimmers and can withstand temperatures far below 0° without discomfort. They can bear the summers blistering heat while other creatures seek out the shade. The bison have a pecking order type of society. This means, simply put, that might is right. Again there are no exceptions.

Now that you have a little background on these magnificent creatures, let's get down to some ranchin' stories. A lot of people, including myself, wonder why in the hell would one of the towns most prominent and successful orthopedic surgeons would want to risk life and limb raising a bunch of wild-assed buffaloes? The conclusion I came to was he loves them, and it is a vent or release from the stress and tension that is a surgeon's life.

By far the most interesting time on the ranch is the calving season. In general bison have little trouble giving birth. What sometimes happens though, for some unknown reason, is occasionally a calf will refuse to nurse, or the mother won't let it nurse, or sometimes the mother dies as a result of birthing. Whatever the reason, you have an orphan calf to deal with. As I mentioned earlier, if the calf does not get the colostrum, it will die. Bison will not adopt another's calf as cattle often will, survival of the fittest again is the rule.

When you have a calf who cant get the colostrum for whatever reason, you basically have two options, shoot it or save it. I always preferred the latter, this however is a dangerous undertaking. The first step is to make sure you have some colostrum on hand. No, you don't milk a bison, you must get it from a dairy. They save it for just that reason for their calves, should a similar fate befall them. If the mother has died, you can extract her milk post mortem, (Dr. talk) and bottle feed the calf with it.

The hard part lies in catching the little buggers. As I mentioned earlier, they can run damn near right out of the chute! When it really gets interesting is when the mother is alive and the calf won't nurse. Our job is to kidnap the calf. This is real dicey work and mistakes can be unforgiving or worse.

The first time I saw this done, Doc went out with the four wheeler and harassed the mother until he got her to give ground. Then he proceeded to move her away from the calf, who was weak and confused, and stayed put. After Doc figured he had moved the mother far enough away from her calf to effect the kidnaping, he drove as fast as he dare back to the calf, so as not to alarm it, dismounted his mechanical horse, and snatched up the calf, got back on the wheeler with the calf in his lap, and prepared to head for the barn.

By now the mother had seen Doc with her calf, and does not like it one bit. Here she comes, charging across the field, mad as hell. Doc sees this and gives the wheeler some gas and the damn thing dies on him! Now Doc, being a surgeon and all, is no dummy and is quick to realize he's in a pickle. Quickly, he runs towards the mother a little ways, sets the calf down and returns to his disabled mechanical horse, wishing like hell he had a real one!

Meanwhile, momma has returned to her calf, gives it a quick once over and turns her attention towards that unruly human nuisance out in the middle of nowhere cowering behind a little four wheeler. It has been said payback is a bitch, and The Doc is about become a believer.

This is about the time I show up at the ranch. At the time, I was still pretty new at this bison ranching stuff, but I could tell there was someplace else Doc would prefer to be. That old gal was butting the wheeler with her head, when I showed up on the tractor and ran her off.

7

With reinforcements on hand we finished the kidnaping, and got the calf back to the barn and fed it some beef colostrum, but our efforts were in vain, it died anyway, as most do. In my four years at the ranch I think only one orphaned calf made it, but we have to try.

Doc is married to a pretty, petite woman named Carol. By looking at Carol, the last place you would expect to see her is out on a bison ranch, but that's where you'll find her, right in the thick of it all. Many is the time she has saved the day, not by brute strength as one might assume is how things get done on a bison ranch, but by out thinking them, she is a master of it.

I've ran my dumb ass ragged trying to chase down them little buggers and gave up in disgust, only to look out to see Carol leading the whole damn bunch of them across an open field by throwing bread down behind her as she walked them right into the corral! One would be foolish to judge Carol by her looks. Get her pissed off and she'll serve you up hell for breakfast, with all the trimmings. Just ask Doc, who bestowed upon her the moniker of "The War Department!"

The day that we all lost sleep over, was inoculation day. This is when we must run the herd into the holding area, down the crowding lane, into the circle. From there into the squeeze chute, where we immobilize and them give them a barrage of shots, tag, and sort them. Then we release them, during this hectic time Murphy's Law is the only certainty.

It should be understood that bison are not like cattle, they are wild animals. When you confine a bison or in any way impinge upon their freedom, all hell breaks loose and you had best be ready to deal with it. The corral fences are built with telephone poles for posts and highway guardrail 8 feet high, and they still try to take it down!

We run them down the crowding lane by means of a big tractor, with a front end loader bucket for a little added persuasion. This too, they try and run through. They are lured into the corral area with bread; Doc and Carol buy reject bread from the bakeries by the ton. It is always more desirable to lead bison than drive them, we learned that from the War Department! Once they are in the compound, a quick startling movement in the direction you want them to go will usually send them on their way. Timeliness in the opening and closing of gates is critical to the mission's success.

Doc heads them down the lane with the tractor, once they are in there, I secure the gate and the fun begins. I was the lane man. I keep them moving towards the squeeze chute, work the circle down and try to

8

keep them from killing each other. They literally go berserk in captivity. The larger animals will gore, kick, and trample the younger, weaker ones. The tools of my trade are a long two by four and a cattle prod. I try not to use the latter very much, but sometimes I must.

My son Eric is the chute man, he squeezes them down and assists the Doc as needed. The War Department keeps the records and helps with the tagging and whatever else needs to be done.

Doc, being the Doctor and all, gives them the shots. Towards the end of my stint on the ranch we running close to a hundred head, that is a good days work. Doc's hands would get cramped up and blistered from giving so many shots. Animals have lost eyes, horns, and a few have died in the process, but it must be done. Though large and robust, parasites and pneumonia can kill a healthy bison in 48 hours.

You must be vigilant in your surveillance of the herd, if an animal is alone by itself, it is sick. Fewer animals have a herding instinct stronger than that of bison. If an animal has a "humped up" posture, it is sick. You must also constantly check their stools, scours must be treated at once. Illness can run rampant and be devastating to a herd.

When an animal was killed for meat, Doc would always allow various Native Americans to come out and perform ceremonies to honor the animals. He was also a supplier to numerous craft persons who made their wares from bison by products, bones, teeth, ribs, skulls, hides, even the scrotum is used for a tobacco pouch!

Although Doc didn't like it to much, I would always name the bison, who I refer to as 'The Boys'. I would choose their name by either a physical or behavioral trait. Doc claimed, that if I named them they didn't taste the same! Every bison ranch must name the patriarch of the herd, Bill, as in Buffalo Bill, and so it was at the ranch. Doc has had old Bill for over twenty years. He was the herd bull for many years, but age has taken its toll on the old boy, as it does on all of Gods creatures. He has lost his standing in the herd, he'll even give ground to an old cow rather than fight anymore.

One time, Doc and I noticed Bill had quite a pronounced limp in his front leg. We guessed he had picked up a rock or a nail in his foot and decided to put him in the chute and have a look see at the old guy. He didn't put up that much of a fight, in fact he's a lot more manageable than some of those old cows. Our exam turned out to be fruitless and we turned him back out in the front pasture where we got him.

We will never know just what the hell started all the ruckus, but as soon as old Bill was back in the pasture, Buster, his son and another big bull, Beaumont, attacked the poor old bastard. They kicked him and ran him until he was tired. Then took him down and began goring him as he lay bellowing helplessly on the ground, they were going to kill him.

My ass they were. I got on the four wheeler, Doc on another piece of equipment and we jumped into the fray in earnest. I was more mobile than Doc on the four wheeler, so I hazed them until finally they relented and took off. Poor old Bill lay on the ground bleeding from several different puncture wounds and had numerous patches of hide missing. The poor old guy was hurtin' for certain. We ran those other two ya-hoos out of that pasture and just left old Bill alone. Soon he was back up on his feet and moving around, not real limber, but at least he was up and about. He would be sore for a couple of weeks, very strange.

When you see bison on TV, often they are in the middle of a stam-pede. Most people aren't aware of what a stampede really is. When bison stampede, they are not headed for any place in particular. For some reason or another they have been spooked and begin to run. The animals at the head of the herd, or the lead animals, are running as fast as they can because they know that if they stop or slow down, they are going to be trampled to death by the mass of thundering beasts behind them. The animals in the rear, see the ones in front are running and assume they are in danger and follow them. Unaware that they are in fact the danger, eventually they will fan out and the mayhem will end; But they never learn. It's instinctual behavior. Native Americans fre-quently used this to their advantage by stampeding them over a cliff, or a 'buffalo jump' as it was called.

A peculiar thing bison do on occasion is what is known as "prong-ing". This when one animal will begin to bounce on all fours, just like a deer does. When the others see this, some are inclined to join in. It is quite a sight to look out and see a bunch of them on the prong. I have concluded, and this is just my opinion from observation, that is a form of play. I've also noticed that it usually occurs during the coming of a new season, most noticeably in the spring and fall.

After watching this a few times, I decided I would join them and see what they thought of me among them. I would get on the four wheeler and get right in middle of a bunch of them, it was spectacular. There was chunks of mud and snot flying around, grunting and roaring, the steam from their breath enveloped me. After about five or so minutes they would just stop and that was it. They'd look at me like I was some kind of an idiot with too much idle time on his hands!

10

Ol' Bill

Cow and Calf

11

GOD BLESS RED NECKS

God bless you jocks and red necks, rebel rousers one and all,
Our country calls on you again, to sound the battle call.
Dry gulched we were old pard, Sunday punched and kicked,
All bets are off, the gloves come off, lo, the fight they've picked.

Let the pacifists and peace nicks, turn their liberal cheek,
They know we'll give our blood again, to save their right to speak.
The lot we've sought are rank and vile, and loathe a people free,
Our duty's clear, as the time draws near, again we cross the sea.

Will the scum that scam the city streets, fight back to back with me?
Will the tie-dyed protesters stand with us, or stay safe up in their tree?
No fears and Bad Boys, unplug your MTV, and lose the cute goatees,
You won't have a boom box in those olive drab Humvees.

Where will the dot com yuppies hide, when the blood runs ankle deep,
Holed up in a penthouse suite, with a bimbo fast asleep?
I'd sooner live with animals, than men with a yellow streak,
Them who won't fight for freedom, have a future dark and bleak.

The good life has a price you know, now the bill's come due,
Our backs are bent, damn near broke, and still we fight for you.
They hit us first and below the belt, now they'll get their war,
Sinister zealots, merchants of death, worship blood and gore.

In pick up trucks with rifle racks, and good old dogs in back,
Red neck justice fresh on tap, pay for a sneak attack.
Holy War, Jihad, they say, run wild and raise such a fuss,
Give your souls to Allah boys, 'cause your ass belongs to us.

THE LOGGER

Born in the high country, wild and steep,
Spry and nimble as a mountain goat;
At home in canyons wide and deep,
Works in the woods, far away and remote.

Beasts of the timber, rugged and lean,
Down right hard to the core.
A full head of steam that's seldom seen,
Never leaves them asking for more.

Cut up, scrapped up, battered and bruised,
Yet still he just won't quit.
It's in your blood, not something you choose,
Tempered in the furnace spit.

He plays in the fog, rain, snow or heat,
It's all just part of his day.
Men strong of back, and tough to beat,
Wade headlong into the fray.

A breed all their own, they go it alone,
They're seldom found in the crowd.
A will of cast iron, a jaw made of stone,
They're men born fierce and proud.

Tight logs and hang ups all day long,
Lines, see-saw, high overhead.
It's Murphy's law, when things go wrong,
One little slip, you could be dead.

Stove up and wore out, by age forty five,
He's lost count of all his stitches;
He's glad as hell, to still be alive,
But it's rags 'n' more rags, to hell with the riches.

DRAWS AND QUITTIN'

If pay day was last Friday, then why am I flat broke,
While the boys are all out guzzlin', at our favorite waterin' hole?
Just like some old sourdough, no dust left in his poke,
I'm prayin' that the boss man, will put me on the dole.

If this outfit won't give a draw, I'll find me one that will,
It's the unwritten code of the woods, if a feller's down and out.
I've got to make the waterin' hole, to lap my share of swill,
Fall in with my logging pards, arm wrestle, drink, and shout.

There's a few things a loggin' man is always gonna do,
Drawing on his paycheck, and quittin' top the list.
They'll just up and quit, when you least expect them to,
There's a few will tell you, what it was that got 'em pissed.

They'll endure inclement weather, brave the danger and the ground,
Bear eternal hours, and the endless crummy rides.
And when they've had enough of it, they'll take a truck to town,
Drink until they're broke again, then call some other sides.

Our crummy rides to and fro, are both made in the dark,
The days are long and hard, 'neath the lines or on the saw.
Every day we live through, is more or less a lark,
But when the pitcher's empty, it's time to get a draw.

A gypo logger knows the code, the rule of quit and draw,
He keeps a checkbook and bottle in his pick up truck.
The code is stern and plain, and its word is took for law,
We take care of our own, when they're down and out of luck.

14

FIRST LOGGING JOB

Being somewhat impatient in my younger days, I had decided that I would forgo the time-honored tradition of working my way up through the ranks and start running equipment, right off the bat. I figured that a skidder was just like a tractor, and I had operated those quite a little bit as a farm hand. With confidence intact, all that remained was to secure employment and begin my career as a logger. The newspaper was chock full of logging jobs, ten or so every day as this was in 1976.

It looked like I would have to tell a little white lie or two to get on a skidder, as all the jobs were for "experienced" men. So I did what I had to do, and got hired over the phone. I hardly slept at all that night, worrying over what I was going to do when it was show time in the morning.

I met the crummy at 5:00 a.m. and off for the woods we headed. I don't think they knew how young I was because it was dark and everyone was hung over and reeked of cheap beer.

Finally we arrived at the landing and the long wait was over. I went right to the machine and started checking oil, etc. trying to look like an old hand, but failing at it miserably.

At long last I found myself sitting in the cab, but something wasn't quite right, there is no steering wheel! This really upset me. What kind of tractor doesn't have a steering wheel for Christ sake? Well, little details like that would have to wait. I started it up and off it went, on full automatic pilot, I was just along for the ride. I was in a state of pure panic and not a clue as to how to steer, much less stop the damn thing!

All of a sudden I had become very popular, I had everyone's undivided attention as I side-swiped the crummy, ran over the lunches, and two chainsaws en route to demolish the fuel cache, consisting of three 55 gallon drums of diesel oil, one of which was ruptured and the other two went for a little "roll". By now there were tin hats flying around like frisbees, arms flailing and more hollering and hub bub than I'd heard in my life...and all for me!

15

Now, right when it looked like I was headed away from everything, she hits a stump and resets her course, dead ahead to the self loader with the owner up in the "roost". Oblivious to what had befallen his landing, but all too soon to be rudely informed! Just before impact something caught his eye, and when he saw me, he immediately let go of the control levers and held on for dear life! Luckily it was a glancing blow, and he kind of crash landed, as opposed to out right falling off! As the skidder tore down the side of the loader the blade hit the outrigger and stopped it in its tracks, killing the engine, and none to soon I might add. My worst nightmare was materializing right before my eyes. I was frozen with terror, and a whole crew of burley, pissed off loggers were bearing down on me fast! Things were not going well at all!

I won't repeat a lot of the things I was called that morning, and I doubt that I will ever forget them either. After removing me from the cab of the skidder and doing a little damage control, I was resolved to set chokers, with no gloves or rain gear for the rest of the day. With no lunch I might add, as I had ran over them!

At the end of the day, the owner got out his check book and paid me $40....($5 per hour) and said he couldn't afford to keep guys like me around! Confidence shattered, with tail between my legs, home I went to face the music, the Old Lady, and her "I told you so's".

Being young and resilient, I was back to my cocky self in no time, and went on to become a very competent skidder operator and all around hand in the brush. It was not an easy thing to do, most worth while endeavors aren't.

MARLIN SPIKE MIKE

Up in the mountains, where the tall timber grows,
There lives a loggin' man, that everybody knows.
He used choker bells, for a rattle as a tyke,
And he roasted marshmallows on a marlin spike.

He gave the school marm a heart attack,
So he learned how to cipher at the riggin' shack.
He kept his britches up with a piece of haywire,
And his favorite toy was a log truck tire.

The first rig he had, was a D-8 cat,
And their family pet was a foot long rat.
He loved to play fetch with a pack of rabid dogs,
And he built a tree fort from old growth logs.

Now Marlin Spike Mike was known far and wide,
To be just a shade on the stupid side.
His sweetheart Myrtle, soon became his spouse,
Her wedding present was a double outhouse.

She had buck-teeth and not a whole lotta sense,
She could eat an ear of corn through a picket fence.
She weren't too tall, but she was just as wide,
He had to grease her hips, to push her inside.

Now Marlin Spike and Myrtle, made the perfect match,
But it made a feller wonder, 'bout the brood they'd hatch.
They had nine kids, they was a homely lot,
So ugly that he fed 'em with his old sling shot.

They had their kids enrolled, down at the reform school,
'Cause they drank all day, and played cards, and pool.
Of the nine in the litter, weren't a keeper in the bunch,
They went to a funeral, poured shine in the punch.

The parson 86'd 'em, from his Sunday school class,
When he got fed up, with their backtalk and sass.
Wherever they would go, there was sure to be a mess,
What they'd pull next was anybody's guess.

They built a lean-to, on the side of a hill,
It was the perfect place for old Granddaddy's still.
They'd come from all over, for his sour mash shine,
Cooked in his shack, 'neath the shadders of the pine.

Now, it's a rough row to hoe, bein' a loggin' man,
But if anyone can do 'er, old Marlin Spike can.
Does he log to live, or does he live to log,
Hell, he don't know, he's just a choker dog.

HELP WANTED

I was thumbing through the paper one day,
When a job add caught my eye.
Wanted: a man to leave, and go far away,
And work a job where he could die.

Don't send us smart ass city boys,
All frail, bent over and sick.
Send us men who've outgrown their toys,
Or we'll break 'em in two like a stick.

We don't want druggies, thieves, or liars,
Send us good men, tried and true.
We'll drag your culls through the briars,
And give them right back to you.

Young men will do just fine,
Send us your brazen and bold.
In time he'll become one of our kind,
If he learns, he may live to get old.

We've had men snap, and wail like babes,
And sent them crawling back to town.
We've put more than a few into early graves,
To spend eternity in the ground.

Wanted: men who are fit and want it all,
Men who don't know fear.
Men to lay down timber tall,
And drink their weight in beer.

Wanted: a few good men to fill our ranks,
Men with guts and grit.
Men as tough as Sherman tanks,
Who don't know how to quit.

THE PROTESTERS

We'd seen 'em on tv before, but thought we was exempt,
From vagabond protesters who've never worked a day.
They wore tie dyed duds and sandals, was ragged and unkempt,
The guys looked like girls, and probably all was gay.

They had corn rows and dread locks, Lordy how they stunk,
They was kickin' little bean bags, and playin' 'round with sticks.
Their leader was a dandy, some skrawny hippie punk,
The women was a motley crew of hairy hippy chicks.

They was chained to our equipment and swingin' in the trees,
"Save the dying old growth" was their mantra and their chant.
They all sang out in unison, "go home you bastards please",
I've tried and tried to see their side, so help me God I can't.

Their doctrine denied prudence, chose anarchy to law,
They liked alfalfa sprouts, tofu, patchouli oil, and pot.
What a bunch of worthless culls, beat all we ever saw,
They never had a clue of the trouble they just bought.

They figured they'd outsmarted us, thought they had us fouled,
It's safe to say that fateful day, they got a big surprise.
When we fired up our chainsaws, they got all scared and howled,
When we started sawing, you shoulda seen their eyes.

We put our locks on their chains, and started up the fire truck,
When we hosed 'em down, they felt the ire of a logger's wrath.
They all shook and shivered, standing in that oozy muck,
But it really wasn't all that bad, at least they got a bath!

WISHFUL THINKIN'

"Wishful thinkin' and whiskey drinkin', is gonna be the death of me yet,
Just how much further in the hole, can one poor ol' gypo get?
If it weren't Monday, I'd swear it was, ain't nothin' gone right since we started,
We've been fightin' hang ups all day long, and the haulback: she just parted."

The very last hour, we pulled down the tower,
And wiped out the whole damn side.
I blew a long and a short, I felt out of sorts,
I threw down my bug, and I damn near cried.

I looked over at Bill, and if looks could kill,
I'd of fell over dead right there.
He looked plumb disgusted, dog tired, and busted,
And a whole lot worse for the wear.

My heart was poundin' faster, what a horrible disaster,
The chips was a flyin' around like confetti;
The tube lay on the ground, tin hats was flying 'round,
The lines was a tangle of steel spaghetti.

The saws got smashed, the crummy was trashed,
The only thing remaining was the fire truck.
She popped and farted, but we got 'er started,
Then backed it in the ditch, and got 'er stuck.

I was bitchin' and a cussin', the crew was a fussin',
I stomped over mad, and fired up the Cat.
I hooked up to that pumper, then yanked off the bumper,
We was screwed to a standstill, and there we sat.

We was soon down the road, atop a three log load,
Headed to town on Peterbilt.
The driver bless his mug, he passed us up a jug,
We done our duty, not a drop got spilt.

"Wishful thinkin' and whiskey drinkin' is gonna be the death of me yet,
Just how much further in the hole can one poor ol' gypo get?
One of these days, I'll change my ways, that is if I don't die first,
But one thing's for certain, come hell or a hurtin', I won't be dying from thirst".

24

WOODROW

I could, and I still might, write a book about Woodrow. Some Hollywood mogul could make a movie about that idiot and it would probably end up as a blockbuster hit. I'd have Woody Harrelson play Woodrow!

Woodrow is not his real name, it's a nick name I bestowed upon him in honor of Captain Woodrow F. Call, member in good standing of the esteemed Texas Rangers. It was a western movie he liked real well called, "Lonesome Dove."

I still call him Woodrow, and he's even had bosses make his check out to 'Woodrow'.

I find myself at a loss as to how to go about telling about him, so I'll engage you in what my sons and I refer to as "remembrances". This is when we're all sitting around chewin' the cud, and it always comes to, "remember when Woodrow did this, that, and the other". We get a big kick out of it, but Woodrow doesn't like it too much, as we are recalling one of his never-ending catastrophes of every imaginable sort. It boggles the mind.

To hear me talk about him, one might get the idea I don't like Woodrow. That's not true, it's just that Woodrow is an idiot, and I try to point it out to him as often as I can!

Woodrow has some good points about him too, they just aren't real noticeable at first glance.

Woodrow is arguably one of the best loggers I've ever seen. The man is fearless, very woods savvy, and has a work ethic born of a time long ago. Woodrow's biggest problem, apart from being an idiot, is and has always been women. You see, Woodrow is a looker and the women really like the little bastard, until they get to know him!

Now, that is not such a bad thing in itself, except for that the women he attracts all seem to have one thing in common, and that is they're all crazy.

I don't use the term loosely either, they are certifiably crazy, with papers to prove it.

The first time I met him, he was the new guy hired onto pull riggin'. He got in the back seat and introduced himself, I thought to myself "oh boy". He had just been in a pretty good scrap recently and looked like he came out on the short end of it. We refer to it in our remembrances as when he got "eighteen-year-olded".

Woodrow had been up in Alaska, tramping around the camps. His not so little wife, Wanda had her fill of it and got herself a boyfriend. An eighteen-year-old boyfriend. Little Wanda was throwing a party for her new boyfriend's eighteenth birthday, and as it turns out, Woodrow coincidentally ends up as the guest of honor. Now ain't that a hoot? The poor fool got beat damn near senseless and lost his front teeth in the melee.

Woodrow always had some sort of trauma going on with his dentures, after he got he finally got them. He's gone through three or four sets that I know of. Each one of them have been super glued, sanded, drilled, buffed and God only knows what else. None of the teeth are even because they've all been knocked out and glued back in!

One time the dumb ass was water skiing and his teeth caught a little too much air. Out they come, in over a hundred feet of water, (dentures don't float). He damn near drowned trying to find them, never did. He wore a motorcycle helmet in public for three days until he got some new ones. It would be an understatement to say that Woodrow is an interesting character. If you want to see him a little more interesting, just add alcohol. After three beers he's a babbling idiot and a disaster in the making. That's usually when the women, (kooks) come into play. One right after the other.

My sons and I give them all nick names. There was The Sorceress, The Tigress, The Slut, The Farmer's Daughter, The Cow Girl, The Fat Lady; and who can forget Ol' One Lung, had one lung and smoked like a house afire! The two that really take the cake are The Judge and The Duck.

As one might surmise, Woodrow's carousing has led to a nearly insurmountable child support bill that he does not believe in paying. The only time he ever makes a payment is to get out of jail, then once sprung he goes back into noncompliance.

In addition to not believing in child support, he doesn't believe in monogamy, (he thinks it's a type of wood) insurance, taxes, traffic laws, and licenses of any kind.

Let's talk about Woodrow's loves. The Judge and The Duck. The first one was The Judge. I won't reveal her real name for fear of being sued, shot, or worse. The poor Judge, bless her little heart, was afflicted with a host of mental troubles. Including, but not limited to; schizophrenia, manic depression, mood swings, and permanent PMS to the degree that she's on some sort of disability because of it. Woodrow said she has a whole shoebox full of medicine she takes for it.

26

The moniker of The Judge I'm afraid came from me. After she made us aware that she has never been, or never will be, wrong about anything, has never made a mistake, and doesn't plan to either.

The Judge would have been a first rate private investigator or detective. She was forever trying to pin dirty deeds on Woodrow, whether he did them or not. Sometimes he would confess guilt, when in fact he was innocent, just to shut her up. Though the truths be known, he was usually guilty as charged. Once The Judge had exacted her confession, all was forgiven, until the next time.

Now in fairness to Her Honor, The Judge, Woodrow has been a pathological liar since he learned to talk, he's lied like a rug when the truth would sound better. It became habit and second nature, sometimes I think he started believing his own lies.

When Woodrow got eighteen-year-olded, he lived in Woodland, Washington. After his cool reception at the birthday party, he set out for greener pastures and wound up in Eugene on his parents' doorstep. When he met The Judge, the dumb ass was embarrassed to tell her that he lived with his parents. So naturally he tells her that his parents live with him because they are a little down on their luck.

Now, The Judge may be crazy, but she's not stupid. With that, he had set the stage for an ongoing investigation that was to span the duration of their relationship of over five years.

When Woodrow and The Judge had a blow up, she would storm off after him screaming, "it's over". These little spats were to become known as "overings", they would be too numerous to count.

At first I felt sorry for the dolt. He would be bawling and all down and out, so I introduced him to my favorite hobby, fishing the high mountain lakes. We would hike into remote mountain lakes for a day or three and troll for big rainbow and brook trout. It would take his feeble mind off of The Judge for a while and proved to be an unending source of entertainment for me!

Woodrow was forever getting himself into a pickle, mostly as a result from his being an idiot, but his chronic impatience always played a big part in the disaster de jour. I have literally doubled over in laughter watching him turn simple, mundane tasks into a hilarious string of calamities worthy of that TV show, "Americas's Funniest Home Videos."

The first time I took him to Devils Lake, I tried to show him the time-honored way of getting into an inflatable raft, without rupturing it, or worse yet, ending up in the drink. I showed him how we put our gear in the raft, then roll up your pants to your knees and walk your boat out into about a foot or so of water, and then you just kind of roll into it and you're off and fishing. He wasted no time informing me that he was a hooktender and didn't need any advice from me. Off he went to a rock ledge to show me how a hooktender does 'er.

I knew better than to try and argue with the fool, so I just went about my business and started fishing, with that tell-tale grin on my face! I hadn't been at it for too long, when I heard a loud splashing noise from Woodrow's locale, followed by a string of obscenities I wouldn't put in print. I spun my boat around, and all I can see is the top of his bald head bobbing around beside his upside down boat. I chortled across the lake to him, how much I appreciated him showing me how a hooktender gets in a raft, but I'd stay with my way.

Woodrow had just gotten a new wallet and it turned all of his money brown. Being an idiot, and not trusting banks, he carried all of his money with him all of the time. He was afraid people would think he was a counterfeiter!

The fool got so cold, that eventually we had to pull the plugs and go out. This really ticked me off because Devils Lake is called Devils Lake for a reason, it is a real chore to get there. It's a mile hike up a steep mountainside, covered with old growth windfalls and you guessed it, lots and lots of devils club, very nasty stuff, and lots of skeeters too.

Then there was the time that we hiked into Raft and Strider Lakes, in a steady Oregon rain and arrived at our destination soaking wet with not much daylight to spare. Hurriedly we gathered our night's supply of firewood and put together an impromptu camp atop a rock ledge over-looking the lake. Soon we had a roaring campfire going, and had erected some makeshift racks to dry our clothes on. Clothing secured on the racks, it is now time to indulge in the tradition of the opening of the fifth of whiskey that is always packed in and began the festivities.

I made a suggestion to Woodrow, that he may want to move his synthetic long johns a little farther away from the fire. Once again I'm chastised and told the virtues of minding my own business and that he knew what he was doing. I just grinned and passed the jug back to him. As the contents of the bottle waned, our spirits soared and soon we are impervious to the elements and bull shittin' up a storm. Woodrow gets up to go shake the dew off his lily, and as he does, he goes sideways as much as he does forward, and his foot catches his little clothes rack and that was all she wrote. His fancy new long johns went up in ball of acrid black smoke right under his nose. Woodrow's son Stan was with us, he and I cracked up laughing so hard that Woodrow got pissed off at us and emptied his Taurus 9mm into the lake. Our ears rang the rest of the night.

Another one of Woodrows more colorful calamities occurred at Bobby Lake, up in the Waldo area of the Cascade range. We had arrived at the trail head around daybreak for the three-mile hike into the lake. This was only a day trip, so we had to be there early to get in all the fishing we could.

After a pleasant stroll to the lake, we sat about airing up our inflatable rafts and rigging up our rods for some trolling. The sky was bluer than blue, and I could tell from experience that it was going to be a hot day. Thinking to myself that I was wasting my time, I told Woodrow not to over-inflate his raft, as it would expand as the air inside of it warmed up from the sun.

As usual I am rebuked, and informed that he is a hooktender, and needs no help from me! And also as usual, I just grin and wait!

Now, I honestly thought that the way it would happen would be with him out on the lake, trolling and it would just expand and blow up with big bang, and dunk his ass. I couldn't wait!

But as fate was to have it, I would be disappointed. With our rafts inflated, we prepared to embark onto the choppy waters of Bobby Lake. In a gesture of defiance, Woodrow kicked his raft and proclaimed, "that's how a hooktender does 'er". At almost the same instant, we hear a whooshing sound, followed by the unmistakable hiss of compressed air escaping! With a look of sheer terror on his face he looks down in disbelief at his raft, flattening out on the ground at his feet!

I tried my very best to control myself, but I just couldn't. I busted up in the most spectacular fit of laughter you could ever imagine! Sound travels very good up at these lakes and in no time we have the attention of the few other people at the lake. Then all at once, Woodrow explodes like a hand grenade in a foot locker. I mean he goes downright berserk! He picks up his oars smashes them against a tree, and reduces them to shards of plastic. Then does likewise with his fishing pole, in a manner fitting of Davy Crocketts last stand at the infamous Alamo. Having dispatched of these implements, he draws his knife and leaps like Tarzan on top of his now deflated raft and attacks it in a fit of pure rage. Needless to say, during all of this he is screaming a string of profanity such as few have ever heard.

At this point, I am literally physically unable to laugh standing up, so I am rolling on the ground as if in a seizure of some kind, laughing uncontrollably. By now we have the undivided attention of any and all persons within earshot of Bobby Lake. Those poor people came all that way to enjoy a day of tranquility in the splendor of the wilderness and they wind up witnessing a psychotic meltdown! They were actually terrified, down right fearing for their lives, packed up their gear, and hiked out as fast as they could!

Seeing this jarred the dumb ass back into reality. He collapses, exhausted, on top of his now shredded raft, and lies panting beneath a cloud of dust and flies in a state of morbid depression. Slowly, I composed myself enough to console my little "not so tightly wrapped" pard and we hiked out and went home. My abdomen ached for days from laughing so hard!

Eventually, The Judge grew tired of Woodrow and moved along. Once again I find Woodrow at my doorstep wanting me to take him fishing. He wants to fish Eastern Brook Lake and find himself amid the wonders of nature, to try and forget The Judge.

I tried my best to talk him out of it, but when he offered to pay for all the gas plus buy my beer, I caved in and off we went. Eastern Brook Lake is not an easy place to get to. First, one must get to Taylor Burn campground. At that time, the last 7 miles were a four wheel drive road and then a two mile hike into the lake. When we got to the campground we set up a quick camp, laid in some wood and then headed for the lake for an afternoon and evening of fishing. We aired up our rafts, and set off in opposite directions in search of lunker brookies.

I could tell the little bastard was hurting because of how quiet he was, so I figured I'd just leave him be and hoped like hell he found himself soon.

When there is no wind, sound travels very well up at those lakes, due in part to their geographic likeness to an amphitheater or bowl. Soon I hear sobs and stifled crying from the opposite end of the lake. After a while I begin making my way towards my broken-hearted little pard. I splash around a bit so he will hear me and compose himself, but he doesn't care if I'm there or not. He's bawling up a storm, wailing about how he lost his little Judge. I try to console him by telling him he should be thankful he got shy of the kook, but this only adds fuel to the fire.

Soon he is nearly hysterical, and howling for The Judge, begging me to scrap our trip and go back and find The Judge so he can renew their love. I knew that any resistance would be futile, so I conceded and we set off for town, hell bent to find The Judge. But it was not meant to be, Woodrow's little Judge had flown the coup. Woodrow would be sad and mourn for a while but soon he would back to his old self and a magnet for another kook....The Duck, more on her later.

RIGGIN' MEN

Riggin' men are born, not made,
'Tis an affliction of the blood.
Not everyone can make the grade,
In the land of eternal rain and mud.

Talkie tooters on their hips,
And stagged off riggin' britches.
A life of endless falls and slips
In and out of muddy ditches.

Wide roads, tag outs, chinee's and swedes,
A riggin' man's seen 'em all.
Day in and out he sweats and bleeds,
"Go right ahead on 'er, boys", they call.

Settin' cork-screwed chokes on big tight logs,
Is like trying to push around a rope.
Hearts of gold, but they smell like hogs,
Gotta sneak up on a bar of soap.

The hooktender has a glass eye, two wooden legs,
And a porcupine for a pet.
For breakfast he eats buzzard eggs,
He's 'bout as tough as a man can get.

His caulk boots are the size of a gun boat,
He's got a chip on his shoulder to match.
He crawls around the hills like a mountain goat,
And he's harder than Hell to catch.

So you think you've got what it takes, to be a riggin' man,
Well, don a tin hat, some caulks, and gloves,
and keep up if you can.
There's a thing or two to keep in mind,
If your plans are to live through the day.
The most important thing, you're gonna find,
Is to keep your ass out of the way!

THE WATERIN' HOLE

'Tis a beacon it is, beaming brilliantly bright,
It's been the salvation, for many a lost soul.
The service commences each Saturday night,
At the wayward order of the Waterin' Hole.

The pulpit's a bar with empties stacked high,
The Parson hears the call of "I'll have another".
He's balding, big bellied, and sports a black eye,
He smokes cheap cigars, but still loves his mother.

No tithing required, nor plate is there passed,
You come as you are, and go as you please.
Ain't no dress code, and no questions are asked,
No sermons recited on sore, bended knees.

The parkin' lot's full, it's standing room only,
It's the best show in town, come one and come all.
The barmaids all shave and most of 'em are homely,
But come closin' time, they all look like a doll.

If fightin's your game, you're at the right place,
There's no line or waiting, just put up your dukes.
You'll get your teeth knocked right from your face,
By red neck maniacs, and a bunch of drunk kooks.

If it's women you're after, you'd best hit the road,
You're at your wit's end, if that is your plan.
Kiss 'em all night, they still look like a toad,
One can hardly tell if they're a woman or man.

There's no phone in the place, the Old Lady can't call,
To cut short the evening and spoil your fun.
There's dozens of pin ups, hung up on the wall,
It's where we pay homage, when our workin' day's done.

33

34

SKIDDER LOGGIN'

Weaving through stumps, and sliding side hill,
Atop my trusty old Triple Six.
Her diesel's a screamin', my God what a thrill,
The brakes are on fire, and I'm in a fix.

The steeper the ground, more is the danger,
Do what we must, to get out the logs.
No job is too tough, for me 'n my Ranger,
And we don't need no choker dogs.

I'll swamp the Chaser and plug the chute,
They won't be waiting on me.
They'll keep up, or I'll give 'em the boot,
That's the way she's gonna be.

An empty choker will fall off for sure,
And they're harder than hell to find.
You look every place, but where they were,
If you look too long, you'll go blind.

The noise will ring in your ears,
For long after quittin' time.
I've kept chiropractors in business for years,
Tinkerin' on my worn out spine.

The battery's dead, there's no starter switch,
And three of her tires go flat.
I've beat so much on the son of a bitch,
I ruined my new tin hat!

They used her once for the haul back block,
They pulled her right over the hill.
She went over twice and lit square on her top,
I'll be damned if she ain't runnin' still.

Runnin' skidders, is hard on a guy,
At least that's what I'm told.
It's a damn good way, to make a grown man cry,
And to turn a young man old.

ALASKAN ADVENTURES

If there is one thing that holds true of traveling and logging in south east Alaska, it would have to be that there is no such thing as "normal". Normality, or any semblance there-of, is left at the airport in Seattle!

Woodrow and I had hired on for this outfit over the phone, and had borrowed against our wages to pay for transportation to get there. Upon our arrival in Seattle we were feeling pretty good, and most of our pocket money was in the hands of the bartender aboard the plane; as per tradition.

When Woodrow and I are in this giddy state, it doesn't take much to amuse us, so you can imagine our reaction when we see this older guy, about 60 something, walking around in the airport in full logging regalia. A regulation loggers outfit by God, and it was immaculate, even starched I think. Atop his head was a chromed tin hat, I shit you not, a chromed tin hat, this was no doubt the man's goin' to town suit, and he was damn proud of it!

Now, you may be wondering what we find so amusing about that. Well, the old boy is packing around a huge watermelon! We could see that our new found friend was under a bit of a strain from hauling that damn thing around, and like the gentleman we were, we offered him a helping hand, which he gladly accepted. After informing us of our fate should we drop it, we assured him we would not and continued on our way to our departure point.

Our conversation revealed that we would be on the same plane. He was going to Ketchican, then on a float plane, out to his logging camp to surprise everyone with a watermelon. He sure as hell would surprise them. When we got aboard the plane, the old boy put his melon in the seat beside him, and put a seat belt on the damn thing!

As we had hoped for, our friend rewarded our good samaritanship with liberal quantities of alcoholic refreshments during the flight from Seattle to Ketchican, where he bade us farewell. We continued on to

Petersburg, and to our new logging jobs in Alaska. Upon our arrival in Petersburg, our spirits were dampened when we learned of a float plane crash the day before, killing all six passengers aboard. Most of them were fellow loggers on their way back to their camp.

We caught a shuttle bus from the airport into town and located the office of our new employer and checked in. That's when things took a turn for the worse. We were informed that there is no camp, and we will be staying at a motel in town, at the expense of the company. This is very unsettling news to us, because it's a well known fact that a logger can't make any money in Alaska while living anywhere near a town. What he makes, he will piss away in the bars.

This opinion, was shared by a few other new guys also, but being damn near broke there's not a whole lot of options open to us at this point. The next morning, a crummy picks us all up for the commute to the job site, this is where things get interesting. After a short drive the crummy stops at a dilapidated, water logged dock in the channel. Here we are instructed to grab our gear and get aboard this run down excuse for a dingy, that should have been and probably was at one time, in Davy Jones' locker. We are told that due to fuel leaks the smoking lamp is out, and upon boarding, each man is given a small pail and told to bail like hell upon request! The old human bilge pump trick.

As the over loaded scow sputtered away from the dock one man was assigned as the lookout. He took his post at the bow of the USS Decrepit and was told to bring to the attention of our esteemed captain, the sighting of any wayward logs or killer whales, (as our captain was legally blind in one eye and couldn't see too well out of the other one).

We weren't very long into our voyage when the command to bail was given to all hands. We eagerly complied, and soon the whole crew was soaking wet and shaking like dogs. We only encountered one Orca en route, and that was from a distance. We just motored over any other obstacles we encountered. After about forty- five minutes we arrived at the opposite side of the channel, at a dock that looked eerily similar to the one we just came from.

Now Woodrow and I were no strangers to the ways of haywire, gypo outfits, we'd been on the hind titty all our lives; but even we were raising our brows at this outfit. Our docking maneuver was more like an amphibious landing than anything else, and no one wasted anytime making for dry land. We were directed to an old school bus, parked on little hump about thirty or forty yards away, told to stow our gear aboard, and then all hands would join together to push start the damn thing. Amazingly enough, it fired up on the first try! We were told to all sit close to the emergency exits and to be ready to use them should the need arise. When we asked if it had bad brakes, they laughed and told us it had no brakes!

By now, Woodrow and I don't quite know what to think of our new job. We half assed expected to find an old steam yarder and spar tree or a team of bulls or something, waiting at our journey's end. We were pleasantly surprised to find a nice little Madill yarder, and a good looking hydraulic shovel, set up on a unit that was just about done being logged. The bad thing being that it was yarding downhill, and a very poor job was done of it. There were logs left everywhere. It was on the last part of one road, maybe a turn or two left, then one road change and that would finish up the unit, except for the clean up, that is.

Woodrow was the hooktender and I was supposed to be the chaser. It was at this juncture that it comes to light, Woodrow and I are the only ones who have any experience in the brush. The yarder engineer and shovel operator knew what they were doing, but that wasn't much help in the brush. The culls couldn't even start up a damn chain saw for shit sake! It was decided that I would be the rigging slinger, and the shovel operator would double up and chase.

The two culls would come out in the brush with me and Woodrow and get a crash course in the fine art of settin' chokers in the mud. One of the culls was a real dingbat, dingier than a shit house rat. His name was Don, we called him "Lap 'em up Don" because he could never get enough water to drink. He had some kind of metabolism problem along with his mental disorders. The dumb bastard would get down on all fours and lap water right out of a mud puddle. We saw the fool lapping out of the top of a fuel barrel, he was a real Jim dandy. He didn't even have any boots. What kind of an idiot, comes up to an Alaskan logging camp in tennis shoes? Lordy, Lordy. We were to find out later, he liked to pull a cork a bit too!

We finished up the tail end of the road we were on, then did a quick road change and were getting ready to start on the last road. Then the shovel operator told us the superintendent had called on the radio, and wanted us to tear down the yarder and get it ready to move to a new locale, and do it pronto.

As we slacked off the guy lines and went out to the stumps to unhook the screwies, we find that most of them are tied back with twisters.

A twister is a method of reinforcing a guy line stump, whose anchorage to the ground is suspected of not being able to withstand the pull soon to be applied to it. To put a twister on a stump, all you do is find another stump near by and take a section of haywire and loop the haywire around the two until you run out of haywire; which is about 250 ft. Then the two eyes are connected, and a small chunk of wood, about four inches in diameter, and around 5 or 6 ft. long is applied in the fashion of a windlass. The purpose being to tighten up the wire connecting the two stumps. After the desired tightness is attained one end of the chunk is dogged into the ground, completing the job.

Putting in a twister is a good way to get the shit knocked out of you if you don't know what you're doing, as is undoing them. As our resident cull, "Lap 'Em Up" was about to find out. This guy was something else. He was one of the few people I've encountered who actually make Woodrow look smart. Woodrow, the idiot that he is, is a top notch logger; one of the best there is.

I had Lap 'Em Up come with me, and Woodrow took the other cull, (who's name I can't recall), with him. As we came to our first twister, I sat about unhooking the screwy, and unbeknownst to me, Lap 'Em Up had taken it upon himself to undo the twister. This fool doesn't have enough sense to undo his bootlaces, hell, he doesn't have enough sense to wear boots!

All of a sudden I heard this thumping sound, followed up by a staccato report of obscenities and howls that could easily be mistaken for a Bigfoot caught in a bear trap. Startled by all the commotion, I wheeled about to catch the tail end of the show. The fool had undogged the twister and the chunk of wood was spinning around like a windmill run amok, just pounding the hell out of him!

After all the tension was relieved, the chunk fell down on top of poor Lap 'Em Up, who lie there on the ground whimpering, and no doubt wondering, what the hell had gotten hold of him!

That was all I needed to see. I sent him to the landing with orders to get in the bus and stay there, or the thumping I'd give him, would make his bout with the twister look like a slap on the wrist!

Woodrow and I had a little pow wow on the side and we decided it was time to move onto greener pastures. So we quit, right there on the spot. We went back to the bus, "borrowed" it, coasted down the hill to start it, and made our way off the mountain, with no brakes, to where the USS Decrepit was moored and pirated it, along with the now, battered and bruised Lap 'Em Up. We made for the mainland and our escape. We sent Lap 'Em Up back across the salty brine, to the bus which we left running, with orders to return to the landing so the rest of the crew would not be stranded, or else!

We slithered back to our motel and proceeded to get drunk and call around the Ketchican area for new jobs. Good ol' Woodrow came through and got us both on at a camp about a 45 minute float plane ride out of Ketchican, where we could start once we got there! Leaving today was out of the question, so we got everything ready for an early departure the next morning and went to the airport to get our tickets to Ketchican. We were informed that we'd be leaving at 9:30 a.m.; if we could get out. If we were socked in by fog they don't fly, period. As I mentioned earlier, a plane had just went down and fog was suspected as the cause of the crash.

We opted to put our faith in the logging Gods and went back into town for some elbow bending at the local watering holes. We returned to our motel around midnight, being sufficiently oiled up and prepared to retire for the evening, when we heard a hell of a commotion in the unit adjoining ours. We looked at each other and exclaimed at the same time, "Lap 'Em Up". We were right on the money, a few minutes later Petersburg's finest arrived; they hauled the drunken, berserk little asshole off to the clink, where he belonged. He had imbibed a little too much and had tipped over, big time. He beat up his roommate, the mild mannered older fellow who was the shovel operator, and then commenced to demolish the room. Everyone was glad to get shy of the little kook, and then they all quit the chicken shit outfit too! We ran into Lap 'Em Up down in the lower 48 a few months later. He showed up at our job as choker setter, in the same tennis shoes! We fired his ass the instant we saw him.

ALASKA FLOAT CAMP

When I told my wife I was Alaska bound,
She said, "you're looney tunes".
"You must not be too tightly wound,
Those crummies have pontoons".

Hundreds of miles away from home,
On an island with eagles and bears.
I'm gettin' too old and fat to roam,
So far away from my easy chairs.

We catch Salmon, crabs, and halibut,
And feed the bears each night.
We drink warm beer for the hell of it,
Hoot 'n holler, laugh and fight.

We live in cabins built on logs,
Towed around by a boat.
All the timber grows in muskeg bogs,
On islands far away remote.

Half the equipment will sputter and spit,
The other half won't start.
I swear every day I'm gonna quit,
But I just don't have the heart.

Up and down the hills we toil,
With hardly any rest.
Upon our shoulders, block and coil,
We go like hell and give our best.

The sun shines when it does they say,
But we ain't seen it yet.
I suppose it will one of these days,
But 'till it does, we'll stay wet.

Well, I've been here for a whole two months,
And I'll admit it's quite a life.
I'm gonna draw my pay, leave at once,
'Cause I miss my little wife.

TRAMPIN'

Three hours we'd ride, six days a week,
In the crummy back and forth.
Ol' Woodrow said, "let's tramp this Geek,
Float a loan, and head up north."

As soon as the plane was in the air,
We drank to our hearts content.
We guzzled away 'till the bar was bare,
And our borrowed money spent.

We danced with glee at the ringing bell,
Down at the Fo'c'sle bar.
No jobs had we, and broke as hell,
But free as a gypsy star.

Reality then hit us hard,
The time had come for work.
Out the back, went me and my pard,
Runnin' from the hotel clerk.

The company paid our way to camp,
Then gave us each a draw.
We showed up and decided to tramp,
'Cause we didn't like what we saw.

Then off on a plane to Ketchican,
One more camp and another chance.
That's the way of a trampin' man,
He's the sum of his own circumstance.

He's hard to predict, harder to keep,
His will isn't even his own.
The earth and its bounty his to reap,
He's born, he lives, and he dies alone.

THE ANIMAL HOUSE

In the islands of the South East,
There's some pretty rowdy places,
Born of ill repute and sorry fame.
Vestiges of the human beast,
Residents of shady places,
Nefarious rapscallions, live up to their name.

I'd heard tales of the Animal House, down in the lower forty-eight,
'Twas the camaraderie of the North Land, that made my heart elate.
I craved the antics, and the escapades, of the men called Timber Tramps,
So I packed my bag, settled my tab, and lit out for the logging camps.

I arrived in fine fashion, it was hard for me to walk,
When I stood, I swayed and waved, and I found it hard to talk.
When I checked into the office, they remarked how much I stunk,
The Side Rod said "to the Animal House, and take the bottom bunk".

"Anything you say", says I, "at last I'm finally here",
As I staggered from his office, I was grinning ear to ear.
It wasn't all that hard to find, like a beacon it shone bright,
The windows, all was busted out, my God it was a sight.

The door was all in pieces, and busted off its hinges,
No doubt it was the casualty, of one to many binges.
I introduced myself around, and they all tipped their beers,
I had hit it off right royally, with my new found peers.

The master of the house, had his head laid on the table,
He said "I'd shake your hand son, but I'm feared that I ain't able".
Rats and mice crawled the floors, and pin ups adorned the walls,
There was drunken loggers everywhere, passed out in the halls.

All night long the beer flowed free, we howled and played with cards,
I felt right at home up there, with all my loggin' pards.
But alas this pomp and revelry, grew old, dim and shady,
So I drew my pay and headed back, to home and my Old Lady.

43

BACK TO THE SOUTH EAST

I'm going back up to the South East again,
Back up to the cedars and old growth spruce.
I'll live in the camps , work out in the rain,
Drink warm beer, and I'll chew lotsa snoose.

There won't be no tv's or women to chase,
Won't be no sirens, jet planes or cars.
I'll wear dirty clothes, grow hair on my face,
Sing Buzz Martin loggin' songs, strum on guitars.

I'll contemplate infinity, through long winter nights,
Try and forget all the reasons I came.
I'll be guest of honor of the northern lights,
Live in a wilderness too wild to tame.

I'll be surrounded by Eagles and big brown bears,
Dodge Killer Whales in deep icy bays.
Just loggin' and drinkin' are my worldly cares,
So help me I've tried, just can't change my ways.

It's salt in the air, the mist, and fog,
It's the muskeg spongy 'neath my feet.
It's the need to be free, and a calling to log,
That keeps me up here, in this cold rain and sleet.

We'll charter a plane and all fly into town,
And head for the place, where anything goes.
We'll hoot and holler, get drunk and fall down,
Revel in squalor in bars that don't close.

I'm gonna stay up here as long as I can,
When I get too old, I'll just stay in camp.
I'm only a small part of God's infinite plan,
But I'm so glad he made me a timber tramp.

MORE ALASKAN ADVENTURES

After Woodrow and I pulled off our escape from The Kook Logging Company of Petersburg, AK, we wound up at nice camp out of Ketchican. We found this place a lot more to our liking.

It was a large, ocean going barge, converted into fully self contained living quarters for a logging camp crew. It had a nice little rec-room with a ping pong table and a TV and VCR so we could watch movies, it had all the amenities of home, with of course, the exception of the Old Lady!

We were sitting up in the rec-room one night after dinner watching a movie, and shootin' the breeze back and forth, as loggers have been known to do, when we heard a hell of a crash coming from the crew berthing area, one deck below the rec-room.

Startled, we all looked at each other with a puzzled look on our mugs, wondering what in the name of Billy B Jeezez was going on. We raced over to the window just in time to see a little desk or writing table kind of thing go sailing through the air. It hit the water with a resounding kersplat, and then went to skipping across the bay like a damned water skier. It began bobbing up and down and then it just disintegrated into so much kindling, and that was that.

Then, directly below us, jumping up and down cussing was who we assumed to be the owner of the now splintered desk. We were to learn later, that the dumb ass had tied a heavy duty monofilament fishing line to it, and was chumming for some bottom fish. As it turned out he was a little more successful than he had anticipated! Speculation ran the gamut from a killer whale to a large halibut, with the latter, more than likely being the culprit. The camp superintendent, then issued a standing order that no more camp furnishings be used for fishing gear!

The next day would prove to be one for the year book. Woodrow and I were split up and put on different jobs, as we were both good all around hands, and they needed a rigging man who knew what he was doing on both sides. As is normally the case, I ended up on the shitty end of the stick, the side I wound up on was a real bitch of a hell hole, steep and as brushy as they come.

Woodrow's side on the other hand was like logging in a state park, as flat as my high school English teacher. He had a hell of a nice guy for his hooktender, while the hooktender I had was a washed up drunk who hacked like a machine gun all day long. He was a real smart ass and thought he was a tough guy, until I offered him the opportunity to show me how tough he was—he mellowed out considerably after that.

The rigging slinger on my side was South East Native Alaskan, whom I'll call Pete. He was a very powerfully built man, with stamina hard to match. This guy could go circles around me, or anyone else on the whole damned island. The only drawback he had, was that he wasn't what you would call, real smart. He should have been a choker setter and that's all. But I wasn't there when they needed a slinger and he got the call. They couldn't very well demote him, and give me his job without causing some bad feelings, so that's the way it was.

This particular unit had some very big old growth spruce on it, some of them were six feet across on the butt. They were heavy, real heavy, we could only send one of them at a time and we had to really watch them on their way up, or we'd be fouled for sure. We had just hooked up a monster, it still had water running out of it so we knew it was going to be a heavy s.o.b. We put two chokers on it to play it safe.

We got in the clear and Pete blew, "go ahead on 'er", and the old Berger snorted and began its laborious task of yarding this behemoth to the landing, I was watching as it approached an abrupt rock out cropping and was puzzled as to why I hadn't heard some whistles. I turned around to see what Pete ol' buddy had on his feeble mind, and there he was with his back to the turn and his pecker in his hand, taking a leak! I quickly tried to blow a stop on my bug, but nothing happened, I was in a dead spot and my signal couldn't get out. I screamed at Pete, who suddenly came back to earth, but it was too late. He couldn't turn loose of his pecker and replace it with his bug fast enough. We heard the yarder lug down and hoped that the engineer would feel a dead hang up and stop. It was not to be, he was in the habit of having to horse big 'uns out, and he wound on it. Ol' Pete, the peter puller, was trying frantically to get to his bug when we heard the yarder lug way down, followed by an odd rattling sound. Then we heard a long and a short whistle; this means quitting time! I knew damn well what had happened.

We couldn't see the tower from our position down in the hole, so we scrambled to a vantage point where we could see the landing, and it wasn't a pretty sight. We had pulled the back three guyline stumps and the tube was listing at about 45 degrees, the only thing that kept it from going completely over was the static guy. Poor Pete, the peter puller, was really shook up and he should have been. That was a very stupid mistake that should not have happened. It would cost him his job, and rightly so.

It would also come to light, upon further investigation, that our hacking hooktender, was not altogether blameless in the outcome of this little fiasco. It was the popular consensus that all three of the stumps that pulled would have been tied back by means of a twister, had a competent hooktender done the job. This fool wouldn't even notch a stump for a guyline or in the back end for a haulback block, he was a complete cull.

The side was down for about a day and a half while things were put back together. It was deemed unfeasible to use anymore stumps for the back guylines, as they were all in rock and had no root systems for an anchorage. This meant that the shovel operator had to make his way back and put in a deadman in lieu of stumps. This guy was the slowest shovel operator I've ever seen, and he looked just like Honest Abe Lincoln. It was sure hard to get good help up in Alaska.

We finally decided that we'd better be heading for home, before one of these fools killed us, and off we went.

48

THE TLINGKIT FROM HELL

We'd just tramped another camp,
When our plane lit, she hit hard.
We'd been out two months, been drunk only once,
So off to the bars, goes me 'n' my pard.

Our bank rolls was burning holes in our pockets,
But we had a cure for that.
We got hung up on a stool, down at the Foc'sle,
And there at the bar we sat.

We were chuggin' 'em down, horsin' around,
Taking turns a ringin' the bell.
The good times we had, soon turned bad,
I was being eyed by the Tlingkit from hell.

She had three teeth in her mouth, one eye was poked out,
She shined like she'd just been greased.
I knew all too well, it would be pure hell,
If she caught me, she'd do as she pleased.

Her lips were gloss red, she looked half dead,
She smelled just about the same;
She offered me heat in winter, shade in the summer,
And she didn't even know my name.

So I was beatin' feet, down Water street,
Going just as fast as I could.
If I could just make the corner, I'd give her the slip,
And ditch the old bitch for good.

I ducked into a bar, not leading by far,
But the old gal was hot on my track.
She was bearing down fast, I'd been had at last,
Then I saw the door out the back.

I made good my escape, avoided my rape,
And to this day I remember well.
That night in the streets of Ketchican,
Fleeing the Tlingkit from hell.

50

ONCE UPON A TIME

Stalwart ghosts of the tall, deep woods,
'Twas not blood, but pitch in their veins.
Memories wane of the mountain and her moods,
And history tells of the little that remains.
Like a harlot she beckoned you to her breast,
And like the fools you were, you came.
The unworthy and weak, she lay to rest,
Right where they fell, in a grave with no name:

I'm still amazed at how driven and crazed,
Were those old loggers from days gone by.
They sweat and bled from the lives they led,
Maybe one in ten could tell you why.
When a man and his pard worked so God awful hard,
And each new day men might die.

They cut old growth stands with long steel bands,
Called 'em misery whips I'm told.
If a man stayed alive 'till he made forty-five,
They said he lived to get old.
And history should write from envy or spite,
Of a breed so daring and bold.

When the cream was gone the teams came on,
They skidded logs down greased plank roads.
The ox and bulls strained from the pulls,
But moved their heavy loads.
Boys with mops, greased planks till they dropped,
Their innocence slowly erodes.

Stock wore yokes hand hewn from oaks,
Rigged with chains and cables.
When one slipped up, it got shot and cut up,
Wound up as steaks on the dinner tables.
And believe it or not, there's a few that thought,
Paul Bunyan came from story book fables.

Then a logger's dream, came power from steam,
The donkey would have its day.
The riggin' clanked, it pulled and yanked,
Men gave their all to make 'er pay.
They roamed and camped quit and tramped,
Like wandering stars weren't meant to stay.

Boilers were fed till they glowed bright red,
Now and again one blew.
They'd get old and rust sure enough bust,
Into a million pieces they flew.
Men would die and never know why,
Hope and pray it wouldn't be you.

Men put spurs into giant firs, then topped 'em,
And did a little dance.
Tops would tip, maybe do a flip, then stab in the ground,
Like a giant lance.
Then down he'd go , none too slow, to one more tree,
And another chance.

Logs were delivered in splash damned rivers, they jammed,
Beached and they rolled.
Men dared not to get, all soaking wet, and shake all day,
Like dogs in the cold.
Braggarts and liars gathered 'round their fires, and laughed all night ,
At the stories they told.

The bunk house life lacked the touch of wife,
And all the frills of the city.
The rats and mice, the ticks and lice, took their toll
And lent to the pity.
After dinner each night, seamed only right, to pull a few corks,
And dance a little ditty.

For months they'd slave, do without and save,
Blow into town and blow it all.
They'd get stiff in the lip, stagger and slip,
When they couldn't walk anymore, they'd crawl.
When the money was gone, time to move on, back to camp,
So sick they could bawl.

They'd just up and quit for the pure hell of it,
Draw their pay and head down the ramp.
They say it takes all kinds, and your sure to find,
A motley crew in a logging camp.
They blow in with the wind and out again,
There's no freer soul, than a timber tramp.

Where steel tracks lay, chugged a Baldwin and Shay,
Laden with their booty of wood.
They crossed mountain canyon with reckless abandon,
To far away places where the big ones stood.
They plugged and chugged, pulled and tugged,
They'd go any place where the loggin' was good.

Now the boilers have chilled, the donkeys stilled,
Their tools and mills, gone to rust and rot
They hustled and bustled, they outlawed and rustled,
Trued and tempered by the battles they fought;
Now their legacy's bereft, by the politically correct,
Though their memory wanes, they won't be forgot.

Stalwart ghosts of the tall deep woods,
'Twas not blood, but pitch in their veins.
Memories wane of the mountain and her moods,
And history tells of the little that remains.
Like a harlot, she beckoned you to her breast,
And like the fools you were, you came.
The unworthy and weak, she lay to rest,
Right where they fell in a grave with no name.

CHOICES

Choices made, are made for good,
Be them good or bad.
Now and again you don't choose,
What you later wish you'd had.

Choices pick the roads you travel,
And rough roads they can be.
Choices can leave you high and dry,
Then turn around and set you free.

One choice makes you happy,
While another makes you sad.
Choices made, are made for good,
Be them good or bad.

Aftermath of choices made,
Can hang around a while.
Call the shots all just right,
You might go out in style.

Though life is still hard at best,
Exciting, but so unsure.
Make a choice to make your life,
Just like you wish it were.

Tally's taken at the pearly gates,
For all the choices had.
Choices made, are made for good,
Be them good or bad.

Choices made, like spoken words,
Can't be taken back.
Take a little time in choices,
Life gives up little slack.

The good ole days were good ole days,
Because of choices made.
Waste not your time trying to find,
The goose that laid the egg.

Still , life's a jolly good gamble,
And nothing's iron clad.
Choices made are made for good,
Be them good or bad.

ATONEMENT

I knew this day would come,
It's only fair I guess.
Something has been bothering me,
I should get it off my chest.

These woods I hold so dear to heart,
For years I've laid to waste.
Far and wide, high and low,
We cut to suit our taste.

Three log loads all day long,
Got thirty trucks one day.
Never paid it to much mind,
That's how I earned my pay.

Seems I've aged a bit, and weathered some,
And I'm a lot worse for the wear.
I didn't even get rich from it,
But I don't really care.

The clear cuts will come back one day,
Should we cut 'em down again?
And is that a call that should be made,
By narrow-minded men?

All things are connected and must use,
Of this earth to live.
But who decides what and how much,
And who says it's theirs to give?

We oughta get this sorted out,
Does no one any good.
So let's cut back on people,
Maybe save a little wood.

SENTINELS

Hark: To those stalwart Sentinels, eye witnesses to the ages,
For centuries they've stood,
Monoliths of wood,
Men wrote history and used them for the pages.

Bowed and bent at the will of the wind, frozen in a shroud of snow,
From a tiny twig,
Into a giant so big,
With patience near eternal, no mortal could know.

Nurtured by the rains, seasoned in the sun, tempered by the elements,
Uncomplaining,
So stately and tall,
But destined to fall,
Treasure all of those remaining.

Jewels in the crown of the mountains, towering o'er the world,
Monarchs standing proud,
Reaching to the clouds,
To all of creation, their grandeur unfurled.

Naked to the moon and stars, in all their brilliance beaming,
Stewards to the land,
Shelter for the man,
Inspiration to all who find themselves dreaming.

58

TIPPING OLD GROWTH

The holding wood creaked, as the hinge pulled,
And side hill she fell.
The noise that big fir made that day,
Was heard clear down in Hell.

The needles and limbs rained down,
For a full five minutes, I'll bet.
And if you think that was something,
You ain't seen nothin' yet.

Hours are spent making beds,
Just for these big boys to lay.
So thick and tall a man can fall,
Just a few in a day.

Some of the ground these monsters grow on,
Is as steep as ground can be.
Oh heavens no, we don't kill 'em,
We're just settin' 'em free.

Rugged men in stagged off pants,
With tin hats upon their heads.
Not a way for the faint of heart,
To earn their daily bread.

Some are tipped with wedge and jacks,
Others pulled over with lines;
The tools we use to take them down,
Change along with the times.

Konks the size of dinner tables,
Limbs as thick as a man.
In the mountains of the Northwest,
Grow the biggest firs in the land.

Four hundred years old or more,
And still their wood is sound.
Drop your saw, and run like hell,
When one of 'em heads for ground.

Now, there's all this controversy,
Should we cut 'em or should we not?
Should we try and live off the wood they give,
Or just let 'em lay there and rot?

It will all work out one day,
Someone will win the battle.
If you can't take the fall from the horse,
You shouldn't be up in the saddle.

WOODROW AND THE DUCK

Getting back to my old logging pard Woodrow. As you recall from an earlier story about Woodrow, his Achilles heel is women, crazy women to be more precise. After the Judge flew the coup, Woodrow played the field for a little while, entertaining his usual assortment of kooks he met at the bars around town. Then one night he met up with The Duck. Now The Duck was not her real name. I won't reveal that, as I could very well have a contract put out on me should I get her too riled up. As you probably have guessed, her nick name was my doing!

When she turned sideways her lips looked like ducks lips, so naturally I coined the moniker of Duck Lips, which in time was shortened to, The Duck.

The Duck was a feisty little Mexican gal who had an interesting occupation. For a while I couldn't get Woodrow to tell me what she did for a living. Finally he succumbed to my relentless badgering and spilled the beans. His latest love was a stripper/escort girl! He was afraid to tell me where she worked because he was worried I would go down and introduce myself and harass her. As I reiterated earlier, Woodrow isn't the smartest guy in class, and in no time I knew where she worked and began my favorite pastime of messing with Woodrow! Now, I never did go down and watch The Duck ply her trade, but Woodrow didn't know that, and I was constantly teasing him about how I just got back from the titty bar watching The Duck parade around naked! This would really get old Woody riled up and I really liked that. Later, I came up with an everyday joke. I would say, Woodrow, have you seen The Duck today? He would of course tell me to go do something to myself which was impossible to do. I would cheerfully retort, "well, everyone else has", and begin a leg slapping fit of laughter that would really piss him off!!

I was truly shocked when the dumbass took her to Las Vegas and married her. Needless to say, his parents weren't real happy about it either.

Woodrow's parents were straight laced, upstanding people and were very uncomfortable at Christmas and other holidays in the company of a "working girl"! I of course, was never at a loss to ask Woodrow as to how were the holidays with the folks?

It seemed that The Duck had trouble getting along with her co strippers from time to time. She kept getting fired for fighting! I guess they would encroach on each others "territory" and the resulting catfight that ensued would end in The Duck getting fired. So, she would move along to the next strip bar, or work for an escort service until things calmed down.

The Duck, unfortunately, had three kids, the poor little bastards. They hated Woodrow because they were spoiled rotten. Everything they were told to do, they told Woodrow or The Duck to go to hell, and worse. That didn't go over to well with Woodrow, they were forever causing him misery. He started calling them 'poopwahs!' This only served to piss them off more and cause more trouble for him. One time one of them got in his truck and took it out of gear and it rolled across the street and took out a stop sign! They would take a brand-new car and have it completely trashed in a week or two. They would be in a public parking lot, pick up rocks and throw them at passing cars, and then give the people the finger! The Duck would then go buy them some ice cream or a pizza. It got to where Woodrow finally wouldn't go anywhere with them.

They could really raise hell in grocery store! When The Duck got pissed off at them, she would give them an ass chewing using every cuss word known to a sailor, and a few new ones!

One time, the Poopwahs were messing around in the back yard and when Woodrow went to start up the gas barbeque it started spewing flames up the side of the house. The dip shit tried to put it out with a garden hose, which only served to spread it more. He had to call the fire department!

Woodrow and The Duck, actually had a joint business venture at one time. They were running an escort service together. Woodrow would take the calls and The Duck would supervise "the Crew". Sometimes Woodrow would even drive his wife to her appointments and wait in the car for her. Now I ask you, is that true love or what?

As you might imagine, Woodrow and The Duck, as a result of their behavior and lifestyles were no strangers to local law enforcement agencies. I can't keep track of all the collect calls I've gotten from those idiots from jail! I would show my concern for their dilemma by laughing at them and hanging up! I'd like to have all money they chumped us out of for collect calls.

In an effort to keep this book somewhat suitable for the whole family I wont get into a lot of their antics. At the present time (2003) Woodrow decided it was time to ditch The Duck and go find himself. So naturally if a man wants to clean up, he heads for New Orleans, Louisiana. He was there for about five months, and the last I heard, he was coming home to his little Duck! Here we go again!!

OCCUPATIONAL HAZARDS

With everything there's pros and cons, and work is no exception,
Be your collar starched and white, or blue and smeared with dirt.
Life is wrought with pitfalls, calls for caution and perception,
Rushing headlong into anything, is bound to get you hurt.

The doctor puts an end to our suffering and pain,
He has the admiration and respect of all his peers.
But some he saves are evil, and his efforts are in vain,
Yet he does as he has sworn, in spite of all his fears.

The lawyer serves the vermin, he claims to earn his fees,
It's the law of the land, that he has sworn to uphold.
But he sways the judge and jury, if he must, on bended knees;
Never gives a second thought, to the bill of goods he sold.

The carpenter builds castles and palaces most grand,
With marbled halls and floors all polished bright.
But with every thing he builds, we lose a little land,
At times he stops to wonder, if what he does is right.

The logger clears the forest, for its lumber and the farms,
Making jobs for other men, to earn their daily bread.
But the woods he dearly loves, he knows his labor harms,
He knows that all the city slickers wish that he were dead.

The soldier has a dirty job, he's trained to maim and kill,
Even in the name of freedom, does that make it right?
But its men just like him, whose blood that he must spill,
They wake him up in terror, in the middle of the night.

The cop is on his beat, while he tries to keep the peace,
But the system turns the thugs, back out on the street.
He wonders if this mayhem is ever gonna cease,
The walls are made of bars, the floors of cold concrete.

The world has never been an easy place to live,
And lo, the perfect job, we're never gonna find.
But everyone alive has a little bit to give,
To make a little easier, the daily bump and grind.

THE MILL

It's been idle for years and sits rusting away,
Just off the path of a well traveled road.
It's disheveled, in shambles, complete disarray,
A long time forgotten, a hobo's abode.

The old wigwam stands guard beside the broken down gate,
The windows and doors are all shot full of holes.
She's lonesome like, foreboding, a victim of fate,
Boarded up and abandoned, deprived of her souls.

The whistles are quiet, the chains are all slack,
The clock in the lunch room, stopped right at noon.
There's men out of work, who'd love to go back,
But they won't be doing it anytime soon.

The pond has dried up, the log dump's bare,
Ain't nothin' worth keeping on the whole damn claim.
The watchman quit, or he just don't care,
No beans in the kettle, who gets the blame?

The A-frame's still standing, but not for much longer,
The parking lot's turned into a dump.
The town is dying, 'stead of growing stronger,
You'll do time these days for making a stump.

Days turn to weeks, and the years pass by,
Long gone are the tavern and the old café.
The times are a changin' as the old timers die,
Another time and era slowly fades away.

THE CHASER

The man who runs the landing has his aches and pains,
It's driven more than one feller, close to being insane.
There's sections to make and eyes to mend,
Ends to buck, and chokers to tend,
And the rain and mud will never end.

One day he's up to the top of the tube,
The next he's covered in tacky lube.
There's always lots of knots and limbs,
And hung up chokers to bruise your shins,
And rounded corks on slick buckskins.

There's saws to sharpen and blocks to grease,
One little slip and you could be deceased .
Up ending chokers and shipping nose bags,
Sawing up wood from old growth snags,
Being proud to wear your riggin' rags.

He puts up with truckers, as they gripe and moan,
Listens to the yarder rumble and groan.
Shackles, screwys, connecters, and straps,
Why, a man could get killed, wearing them chaps,
Eatin' in the rain, with lunch in our laps.

Rig up or tear down, it's all the same,
The day we do it, it's gonna rain.
Cramped up and aching from pulling haywire,
But there's no time to sit, by the warming fire,
It's time to go home, and we've got a flat tire.

GRAB ASSIN' AROUND

Horseplay and practical jokes are known as "grab assin' around" and are tolerated in the brush so long as safety and production aren't compromised too much! As a general rule, a man who couldn't laugh at himself or take a ribbing from the crew didn't fare to well in the brush, and should be a truck driver!

One particular incident that comes to mind was a stunt that I used to pull on cat skinners and skidder operators when I was a chaser. It was expected of the chaser to build and maintain a warming fire on cold days. Some outfits had what's known as a salamander. This is a diesel heater, and works all right I suppose, but I preferred a fire, and usually kept a pretty good one going. As the machines would bring in a turn of logs, I would hold up my Stanley thermos and motion them in for a cup and a bullshit session. One guy I'll never forget is Gary "Wide Open" Olsen. Olsen was running a Cat at the time and still lives in Sweet Home, Oregon, he is still a good friend—except that he turned into a truck driver! He claimed "chokers didn't fit his hands anymore". That's all right, I forgave him!

As Mr. Olsen would leave the fireside to return to his machine and resume logging, I would very deftly place a burning cigarette butt in his back pocket. He'd haul himself back up on the Cat and off he'd go, like a house afire and not a clue!

He'd find out soon enough though. All the sudden he'd back off the throttle and the nose of the Cat would dip down, and Old Olsen bailed out the roost patting his fat ass for all he was worth! His hanky would be smoldering and burning, God that was funny!! Only thing was, Olsen didn't think it was too funny! He'd put his "ass fire" out then get back up on his Cat. As he returned with another turn of logs, he dropped the blade down and dozed mud on my warming fire! The s.o.b.!

Then after we ate lunch, I took leave to "see a man about a horse", (go potty) I sneaked over to his Cat and took all the control knobs and related stuff off and piled them in the seat! It took the dumb ass a half an hour to put it all back together! That was all real funny except that unbeknownst to me while I was sabotaging his Cat, he was taking my chainsaws to pieces. Then they brought in all the limbs and broken ends they could find! They buried me in them and I never got caught up the rest of the day!

And there's always the good ole grease gun in the gloves trick! Oh, the things a creative and devilish mind can do with a little tacky lube!

There was this yarder engineer, I called him "Starvin' Marvin". Marvin was a little on the finicky side, a neat and organized type of feller, which is alright with me 'cause there's all kinds of things I could do to him to get him pissed off! Marvin turned out to be quite the prankster himself and we later formed a gentleman's agreement that our talents would be put to better use by making life miserable for the rest of the crew, and spare each other… in other words, I had met my match with Starvin' Marvin!

Marvin was the owner's son, and when the old man wanted something, he got it… pronto! Not just from Marvin, from the whole crew, even the truck drivers turned to when the old man got to squawkin too much! This particular landing was a gummy mud hole, and finicky Marvin didn't like that. I did, just because he didn't! I was the chaser and I'm the one who had to spend all day in the crap. Marvin was up in the cab of the yarder all warm and dry watching me wallow in it. Marvin cut off a bunch of lily pads for steps, they were about 18" in diameter and 3 or 4 inches deep. He had about a dozen or so laid out in a little path to the road. Old Marvin was real proud of that walkway, and it was a good idea, as the mud was a good foot deep, a real mess.

One morning after the trucks were loaded out, I banged on the door of the yarder with my branding hammer and looking real serious. I told him that the Old Man wanted him, and on the double. When the poor bastard got to the ground, I had chopped up his walk way into kindling! He knew immediately who was at work and assured me he would have his revenge, and off he went to deal with the much feared Old Man! As he left, I climbed up in the yarder and drew mustaches on all of his pictures of his wife and kids! I was a real hit with old Marvin! Later in the day he filled up my vest pockets with log branding paint, Forest Service yellow, and before I realized it was in there, I got it all over the crummy and everywhere else! This really got the Old Man pissed off, and he advised us that the grab ass had better quit, and it did! For a little while.

68

Another incident that comes to mind is that of a little trick I played on a particularly annoying yarder engineer. This man was given and lived up to the not so sought after moniker of "The Prick". A genuine smart ass he was.

The only reason he never got his ass kicked on a regular basis was his age. He was in his early sixties and none of us young bucks would have nothing doing with beating up on a senior citizen.

The hell of it was, the old bastard was always right! He had been around awhile and knew more than the rest of us put together, but he had a real condescending demeanor about him.

One day, having a little too much time on my hands, I got this nice soft cedar limb and set to carving up a statue of our beloved "prick" life like in every detail and to scale!

When my masterpiece was done, I waited until he was distracted and then covertly slipped his likeness into his thermos of coffee that he kept by the door and went about my work, keeping one eye on the "prick"!

At long last the moment of truth arrives, with a practiced hand the cup is unscrewed, removed and placed on the instrument panel, next the cap is unscrewed, removed, and the bottle wafted to savor the contents. Then, and only then is the nectar poured. Only this time something is a little different! When the cap comes off, my little work of art shoots up out of that thermos jug like a Polaris missile and then just kind of bobs around! This poor bastard can't believe he's seeing what he's seeing!

He is jarred back to reality by my uncontrollable caterwauling and carrying on, as this is as good as it gets as far as I'm concerned.

He just starred at it for the longest time and I knew that he was gonna be pissed, I was worried I might have to cuff the old guy if he got to carried away with my ass chewing.

After what seemed an eternity, he looked at me and just busted out laughing. I was very relieved that he took it so well! He hopped out of the cab and asked me how I'd like to spend the rest of today and half of tomorrow trying to remove it from my ass! I told the old bastard to finish up his lunch first because he was gonna be at it a while!

THE TINHORN

I rolled into the crummy stop, the usual time that morn,
To get my riggin' crew, and one new guy.
He was standing in the rain, looking sad and all forlorn,
He was shiverin' and just about to cry.
He wore polyester stay pressed slacks, no rain gear, gloves, or hat,
Had tennis shoes upon his dainty feet.
I wished that I was dreaming, I turned my head and spat,
"Lad" says I, "you're in for quite a treat".

We put him in the crummy, in the back seat with the tools,
In the mirror I saw the terror in his face.
I'll bet that Tinhorn thought we was a bunch of redneck fools,
His eyes was glazed, and fixed towards outer space.
A skiff of snow lay on the ground, the trees all glistened white,
The wind was blowing hard, it hurt our ears.
I told him watch out for the haulback, and stay out of the bite,
You're the greenest thing I've had out here in years.

He couldn't pack a section, nor shoulder up a block,
Spent more time on his ass, than on his feet.
His stay pressed slacks got shredded, he could barely walk,
The names I called that cull I won't repeat.
We were in a pumpkin patch, old growth big and fat,
We dug our choker holes with TNT.
The Tinhorn didn't like that much, so on a stump he sat,
He was always in the way, so we just let him be.

The day was almost over, and the weather getting worse,
The Tinhorn gave 'er up sometime ago;
He was stretched out in the crummy, a bawlin' for a nurse,
His spirit had been broken, and his heart was full of woe.
The Tinhorn never said a word, the whole ride back to town,
His body was a mass of lumps and cuts.
I felt the leer of his icy stare, and saw his face in frown,
But at least he's still alive to hate our guts.

71

CHISEL BIT CHUCK

Hop up on your stools,
You beer guzzlin' fools,
I'm gonna tell you the tale of a loggin' man,

He was born in cork boots,
To a pair of old coots,
In the hills outside of Ketchican.

Known as Chisel Bit Chuck,
He'd fall and he'd buck,
Old growth timber 'till the cows come home.

He was a timber tramp,
He was the beer chuggin' champ,
All around the South East he would roam.

The best friend that he had, was a grizzly bear,
He was hard on the eyes, but a hell of a man.
His lean weathered face was covered in hair,
When the others can't cut 'er, old Chisel Bit can.

You'll find him in the wilds, where the big ones grow,
He was too free a spirit for burden of spouse.
Dodging widow makers, when the cold winds blow,
He reveled in the rancor of an old bunk house.

The best of the best, of the warriors of the west,
He swayed and swaggered some when he walked.
He was hard steel, had a barrel for a chest,
He stuttered and slobbered some when he talked.

He travels in the bays, among the Killer Whales,
As he makes his way from camp to camp.
And he spins his yarns and tells his tales,
He's Chisel Bit Chuck the timber tramp.

THE FIGHT

There's a place you know, where the loggers go,
The floors were all covered in dirt.
Non loggers would never show,
Was a good place, for 'em to get hurt.

No live bands would play there,
So they got 'em an old juke box.
They shot the damn thing full of holes,
And they pelted it with rocks.

The owner one day, stood up to say,
He'd have a disco D. J. that night.
That's when me and Wide Open Olsen,
Decided to stage us a fight.

We planned with care our big affair,
'Twas a shaving cream pie in the face.
Our plan came off with much fanfare,
It was a pure and utter disgrace.

Well, that D.J. feller didn't take it to well,
Fact is, he got madder 'n hell.
There was shaving cream all over his gear,
And all over him as well.

We got the whole place all worked up,
It was quite a sight to see.
The night that disco died in Sweet Home,
Thanks to Wide Open Olsen and me.

CHOKER DOGS HATE TIGHT LOGS

Choker dogs hate tight logs,
To this I will attest.
They root around all day like hogs,
With hardly any rest.

On ground too steep or pancake flat,
Don't matter much to me.
Big old growths, nice 'n' fat,
But tight as they can be.

If there's a log that's nice and high,
As easy as you please.
Check it out with a wary eye,
She's probably full of bees.

Half the time they're on the rocks,
Or laying in a bog.
Why I'd eat my dirty socks,
If I got a nice high log.

Wet limbs slap your face,
And glue your eyes with sap.
And when you find an easy place,
That's where a cutter took a crap!

76

LOG TRUCKERS

Log truckers are a special breed,
Not ordinary folks,
Their office is a Peterbilt, Kenworth, or a Mack.
You'll hear 'em on the c.b.'s,
Tellin' stories, lies, and jokes,
Barrelin' down the highway, seldom looking back.

They Jake Brake down the mountains,
In a roiling cloud of dust,
They get their logs to the mill, no matter what it takes.
They brave summer's searing heat,
The winter's icy crust,
And watch the smoke in the mirrors, burning off the brakes.

They back between the log decks,
Load beneath the towers,
Throw their wrappers, in a driving rain.
They face the highways dangers,
The never ending hours,
Their backs are bad, and keep them in a constant state of pain.

Their bellies rub the steering wheel,
They smoke and chew too much,
They're always quick to gripe and moan and bitch.
They drive too fast and reckless,
They chatter up the clutch,
And they've been known to put 'er in the ditch.

A gear shift is their scepter,
A cheater bar their wand,
They're cab's a tangled mess of sparkin' wires.
Log Truckers all are brothers,
And they share a common bond,
They've all got little hammers, and they like to beat on tires.

They're out of bed each morning,
Long before the sun,
Cruising down the highway's lonesome lanes.
But haulin' logs is dangerous work,
And not for everyone,
Most of them will tell you, they've got Diesel in their veins.

THE BEE STING

We were logging a sale called "Freeze Out" very high up in the Cascades, east of Sweet Home, Oregon. It was beautiful timber, fir, hemlock, and spruce. Very big stuff, some real "riggin' busters" one log turns and dynamiting choker holes was the norm. Three log loads left the landing every 15 minutes.

This was one of those rare instances that fate alone had assembled the near perfect crew—good loggers and good friends to the man. Our shovel operator was old Charley. Now Charley was not a big man but he was stocky, and a real looker. The ladies really took a shine to old Charley, being of Italian descent he had that air of confidence about him.

Now ol' Charley had a few other virtues about him. I'm not sure if his ethnicity had anything to do with it or not. Quite frankly I've devoted enough time wondering about it. When old Charley got the urge to go, he went, I mean he took care of "business" right then and there, no matter the crowd, it didn't faze him a bit! This is considered crass behavior even for loggers!

None the less, we had become as accustomed to that sort of thing as one can. So when we looked up from putting a long splice in the haulback, and there was old Charley atop an old growth stump the size of a dinner table, in all his glory just a pissin' in the wind with not a care in the world—we thought nothing of it.

We didn't need the little son of a bitch anyway, so we carried on with our task and left Charley to himself. We were driving in the spikes and all of the sudden the whole world came alive with the most horrible screaming a man could ever imagine. "Oh God ... oh God ... Help me boys ... help me", he was wailing. "Jesus Christ Charley, what in the name of Sam hell is the matter with you?" hollered Dave, the hook tender.

"Oh God ... Oh God, Dave help me, I got a bee sting on my pecker!"

78

"Well it's no damn wonder" retorted Dave, unsympathetically.

"Take me to town boys, take me in … please boys, please," he pleaded. Seeing as how it was payday, and a Friday and only an hour or so left, Dave blew a long and a short whistle, (quitting time) and we headed for Sweet Home on the fly.

Now poor ole Charley wasn't a lovin' 'er too much during the ride in. Shit, we were an hour and a half out and he had such a grip on his pecker I thought he was gonna pull the little bastard right off. Hoping to distract poor Charley from his agony, Dave was telling him of an old Indian cure for bee stings and the like, "buttermilk, you little goof ball son of a bitch, you gotta soak your little pea shooter in buttermilk." "I'll do 'er Dave, I'll do 'er, just get me to town and I'll get me some, and I'll soak 'er real good." After much ado and in record time, we came roaring into the parking lot of the Chateau restaurant on the east end of town.

Dispatching with niceties and fanfare, we tried as best we could to compose our fallen comrade and sent him inside for the ancient cure of a buttermilk poultice of sorts. Sheepishly, Charley approached the counter and asked the waitress for a cup of buttermilk, trying not to draw too much attention to his predicament.

The waitress complied with his request, but cast a sideways look over her glasses as Charley slipped into the men's room, buttermilk in hand.

Old Charley was standing in the stall soaking his throbbing little pecker in the cup of buttermilk and thinking to himself how smart Dave was for telling him about the buttermilk, when he heard a creaking sound behind him. Startled he turned to find the red faced waitress standing in the doorway. She being a bit startled herself, quickly turned away and headed out the door, exclaiming that she had "always wondered how you fellers reloaded those things!"

THE RITUAL

It's here, it's here, it's finally here,
The day we've all long dreamed about.
That magic, special time of year,
When men go mad in search of trout.

Dust off the creel and tackle box,
Rig up those rods and reels.
Big rainbow trout, as sly as a fox,
A six-year-old hot on your heels.

Dreams are best, no sleep tonight,
Nor daylight spare to burn.
It's fishing time and the world's all right,
Time for the boy to have his turn.

Fog and mist of a cool spring morn,
A wind that's sharp as a knife.
Far off call of the geese forlorn,
Memories made to last a life.

A bond is made with that first fish,
A bill come due, not meant to pay.
See the faith in a young boys wish,
Take him where the big ones lay.

That first fish caught, is never forgot,
The sights, the smells, the scales and slime.
Some of life's lessons need not be taught,
Like old dogs, grandpas, and fishin' time.

TROUT

It's hard for me to even think about,
A world that doesn't have any trout.
Big rainbows in rivers cold and swift,
Time spent among them, forever a gift.

Salmon and steelhead, in the coastal streams,
Wait for their turn, in someone's dreams.
The big macs and lakers, of Cresent and Odell,
How do we thank them, for the stories we tell?

And what of the brookies in high mountain lakes,
Baked 'neath the coals, what a feast he makes.
All alone in the woods, with the eagles and bears,
In my own little world, without any cares.

Cutthroats abound in steep mountain creeks,
Fed from snow melt of near by peaks.
A man with a fish on the end of his line,
Is a man with no troubles on his mind.

On swift river currents I offer my flies,
On clear mountain lakes mirroring blue skies.
My favorite way to while away the times,
Is fishing for trout, and writing these rhymes.

82

BEARS

All along the river bank,
Bears seek the Salmon that they crave.
Winter spent cold, dark and dank
Fast asleep, inside their cave.
From their slumber, spring arouses,
Bears emerge from rocky houses.
Off she goes in search of grubs,
Has in tow, her rowdy cubs.

Wild and free as God intended,
Comical and agile brutes.
High in trees they climb suspended,
Honey lovin' big galutes.
Bears clown around for us to see,
Roam the rivers wild and free.
Raging rivers full to brim,
Shaggy bruins love to swim.

Curious clowns, robust then lazy,
Monarch, of his vast domain.
Drunk on grandeur, gone half crazy,
Loves the blowing wind and rain.
Bears are beautiful, each one's a blessing,
Romping o'er the rocky stairs.
Jesters of the wilderness, keep you guessing,
I prefer to people, the company of bears.

ICE CAPADES

Shortly before I began my logging career, a good friend and I decided we were going to do some winter time fishing, through the ice no less.

It was decided that our destination would be Blue Lake, a beautiful little high mountain lake about 4,000 ft. in elevation, some forty miles east of Oakridge, Oregon. It was only a mile or so hike on a good trail, as we recalled from a trip there that summer. My friend, whom to this day I still refer to as 'Bushwack' and I, ('Backwoods') were avid hunter/ fishermen and pretty savvy about the woods and all, so we figured we were more than up to a little walk in the snow. We left Eugene bright and early in my 1957 Chevy pick up. She had a worn out six cylinder, no heater, and one hell of a bad exhaust leak. It was so bad we had to drive with the windows down.

Being the astute planners that we were, we had stopped in Oakridge and got plenty of worms, some grub, and two quarts of Olympia beer a piece to put in the snow bank and await our return from the lake.

In a day that would turn out to hold many surprises, the first one was to round a bend and look out across a very broad expanse. It was in fact, one of those notorious clear cuts, you could see the scar of a fresh slide on the mountain about a thousand or so feet above us. This was about two miles before where we had anticipated to be stopped by the snow. Undaunted we carried on.

We drove the old girl as far as she would go, turned around, and parked where she would be out of harms way and aimed downhill, just in case the battery was dead, as was sometimes the case.

We set out on foot in snow shoes for that little jewel of the Cascades, Blue Lake. We dallied on in high spirits, unknowingly regaling in our youth.

Our destination, we figured was about a five mile hike. After we'd gone a few miles we came to a bunch of large rocks in the road, and elected to take a breather. Bushwack rolled a big one down the hill and we watched it hurl and bound its way to its demise.

We thought that was pretty cool and set out in earnest, tumbling boulders off that cliff. We marveled at seeing, and hearing them out of sync as they leapt further away. You could see them crash into trees and other rocks and literally explode, and not hear the noise for a couple of seconds.

We chucked every rock we could find off that cliff. Later we wished we had saved our energy. The weather couldn't have been nicer, it was a beautiful crisp winter day. Neither of us had ever seen a sky so blue or had the sense to bring along a pair of sunglasses to go with it, and all that pretty snow. The higher we got, the more of a pain in the ass all of that pretty snow became. When we finally got to Blue Lake we were in about four feet of snow, six feet in some spots. The lake was perfect, just as we had expected. It was frozen over except for where the creek ran in and kept the water moving.

We both knew we were in for some hot fishing on ice! In a frenzy we shed our packs and inflated our rubber raft that we would use for safety while out on the ice. Before setting out on the lake we had a bite to eat, nothing tastes as good as cheese, crackers, and sardines do on a fishing trip.

Once out on the ice it comes to light that we're not that good of planners after all. We have nothing to break the ice with, (no pun intended). In desperation we improvise and fashion one of Bushwacks aluminum oars into a not quite regulation ice hole making tool and went to chopping holes. We made our way to the far end of the lake, where the creek and a little open water were.

Just as we had thought, the fishing was hot, (no poem intended)! We were slaying 'em, rainbows and brookies, beautiful fish about twelve to fourteen inches long, and nice and fat. We would pull a few out, kill them and leave them on the ice for retrieval on our way out.

We soon find ourselves shedding clothing, as the sun got higher, it got warmer. Later in the day, it was actually so hot that Bushwack and I decide we will seize the moment, strip down to our boxer shorts and continue fishing. We were really catching the hell out of 'em.

After a few hours of fishing through ice holes we made our way to the open part of the lake, still out on the ice casting towards the shore. The fishing was good there too, and by and by I hooked into a pretty good sized one. This one wasn't going to give up without a fight. Under the ice and back towards me he came, taking out quite a bit of line out as he ran. He sawed the line into the ice pretty good, I was hung up good!

I was concerned about my line breaking and losing this beauty, so Bushwack suggests I get in the raft and paddle towards shore and pull him out from that way. Not having a better idea, I agreed, handed Bushwack my pole and got in the boat. I got my pole back, and the remaining oar, and set out to land that trout. He eventually grew tired and succumbed to the rod. I finally got him along side the raft and got a glimpse of him. He's a big brookie about 18 or so inches long and he's ready to land. I get reeled up enough, to lean over and grab him, and notice my raft is getting a little soft. The side dipped under the water and some got into the raft. You don't know what pain is until you immerse your badly sunburned balls into ice water. There's really nothing quite like it!

I could hear my screams echo around in the amphitheater like bowl the lake was nestled in. My screams are soon drowned out by Bushwacks caterwauling and leg slapping at my plight. It was at this juncture it dawns on us that we are both pretty badly sunburned, (now might be a good time to interject a warning on the dangers of ice fishing in your boxer shorts).

Our conclusion was that the sun had hit the ice and reflected up, roasting our dadburned balls while we were fishing. Our legs, backs, shoulders, and arms, all the same, and we still had five miles to go to the truck.

Then on a sudden it got darker and colder, as if a switch were thrown. The sun sank beneath the tree line prompting us to look at a watch for the first time all day. We had an hour and a half of day light left, and a bit over three hours of hiking to go, or so we thought.

After a few minutes of chastising ourselves and each other we gathered up our remaining gear, stowed it in the raft and headed back across the lake to gather up our fish, dragging the raft behind us on the ice. As we approach our first ice hole we are surprised to see something moving from afar. Surely the fish could not still be alive, it had been a few hours since we "killed" them. Curiosity aroused, we quicken our pace and arrive just in time to see a pair of camp robbers, or whiskey jays if you prefer, finishing off the last of our fish, then noisily flying off as if to scold us for rushing their meal. All that remained was a red stain and a few bones. It was pretty much the same at each of the remaining ice holes. Feast, or famine, goes the way of the beast. Win some, lose some we figured, and on we went to shore and the trail back to the world.

Once we got to the trail, we got our clothes gathered up and began the agony of dressing. Our levis were semi frozen, like cold tin pants.

Somewhere among the chaos and hub bub I had developed the toothache from hell, and it was here with a vengeance, we were a lovin' 'er now.

All that remained was to fold up the raft, pack it, and we'd be on our way back to civilization and our two quarts of Olympia beer. It turns out that rubber rafts when they get cold, are stiffer than a honeymoon peter! We even considered leaving it, but our ethics forbade it.

Eventually, we reduce it to manageable size and crudely affix it to a pack, and we're on the trail headed for the truck. Every step is torture and the pack straps feel like lashes from a whip every time they tug. I find a little solace, in that my toothache helps to distract me from the agony of my sunburn, and on we trudge.

Soon day gives way to night, and our trail is illuminated by a full moon and the company of stars. We felt as if we were the only two people on earth amid all that silence and space. Bushwack and I had, and still do have a very unique relationship. That is to say we each believe that when you see something that is beyond words, words can only distract you from it.

We have spent many hours on the trail together without a word spoken, yet shared the whole day in good spirits, then laughed all night long.

Such was the way it was on that night. Each of us in our own misery and glory at the same time in that frozen silent wilderness wishing it were over, and at the same time praying it never ends, we'd tasted defeat, but triumphed in the end.

We were both relieved to find our Truck and Olys intact, that's about the only thing that went right the whole damn day!

ELK

Majestic monarchs of their forest domain,
Donning their antlers stately and proud.
Primeval bugling, claiming his reign,
Far removed, from the noise of the crowd.

Forever their right to roam free as the breeze,
Taking their place, in the scheme of all things.
Flitting like ghosts, amid rocks and the trees,
Over mountains and canyons, where solitude rings.

Robust in their body, they've eyes like an eagle,
The will to go on, with time on their side.
Devotion enduring, and a spirit nigh regal,
So sure of themselves, steadfast in their pride.

The staple of ancients, now part of the past,
A piece of our history, that can't be forgot.
Coursing his bailiwick, forthright and fast,
Victor of battles, so gallantly fought.

Gracing the walls of the sportsmen's den,
Or romping through evergreen forests with ease.
Lounging and grazing in the lush mountain fen,
With spirit unbridled and no one to please.

OSPREY

I've a friend who's a fisherman,
He goes most every day.
When he gets his hooks in one,
It seldom gets away.

My friend has wings to float upon,
And talons are his hooks.
He fishes all the mountain lakes,
He catches them in brooks.

He sits on limbs or rests on wings,
As he casts his wary eye.
What a fool, he must think of me,
As I float my little fly.

From the sky he falls head first,
Into the water with a blast.
Beautiful bird, how I envy you,
I've grown too tired to cast.

Noble one so swift and sure,
Forever free and proud.
What a treat it must be,
To live among the clouds.

THE HUNT

He hides in the forest, where it's dark and damp,
The velvet's all gone, and his neck is on the swell;
He peers through the trees as they set up camp,
There's an odor on the air he remembers well.

It happens every year, just before the snow flies,
There's a rustle on the breeze and the wind's got a bite.
The leaves flutter down, and geese fill the skies,
And everyone's got a big buck in their sight.

The Moon's high in the sky, and the stars are all out,
The cork's been pulled, and the bottle passed around.
The campfire dances as they holler and shout,
Hung over in the morning, there's snow on the ground.

There's tracks everywhere, but not a buck is seen,
There's lots of trout willing, in the swift little brook.
The old buck is wary, his senses honed keen,
He'd have his place in the record book.

Time is running out, and there's a quickened pace,
Hunting every day, not a tag filled yet.
The old buck slips away, with a grin upon his face,
Another year goes by, no one claims the bet.

The sky's getting dark, and the snow begins to fall,
The guns are unloaded and they call it a day.
The hunter has to stop, and answer nature's call,
Up jumps the buck, and it bounces away.

But the time is never wasted, get a buck or not,
Deer huntin's good, as long as you can dream.
And far across the canyon, there echoes a shot,
But the trout are still willing in the swift little stream.

FISH ON

I waded and hiked, I prayed and I wished,
All day long, I fished and I fished.
The weather was foul, the rain lashed down,
I'd lost count of the worms I 'd drowned.
I felt some despair, it just wasn't fair, all my efforts, it seemed were in vain,
My depression set in, then ill blew the wind, incessantly down came the torrents of rain.

Alas I resolved that I would be skunked,
My chins were bruised, I'd been battered and dunked.
I accepted defeat, with defiant chagrin,
Another fine fix, I'd got myself in.
Short grew the day, what more could I say, soon I would have to pack up and leave;
My race was run, and the dragon had won, going home fishless was hard to believe.

I told myself, just one final cast,
One more chance would be my last.
With a mighty whip, I let fly my bait,
Resigning myself to deal with fate.
Then came the crash, and a silvery flash, my reel was smoking, and singing like mad,
The fierceness he wrought, my God how he fought, he brought to the fray all that he had.

He ran upstream, then back down again,
It was give and take, lose and then gain.
Spirit undaunted, he fought with out fear,
In a fight for his life, he battered my gear.
On the fight raged, like a mad lion caged, this warrior displayed his courage and grit,
He ran and then lunged, he dove and he plunged, with fervor he fought showing his wit.

I thought to myself, "when will he tire?"
As he fought on, with wanton desire.
My body was aching, burning and strained,
On we battled, as it blew and it rained.
At long last he wavered, sweet victory I savored, the tide of battle finally had turned,
He gave up some ground, I felt my heart pound, the water beneath me boiled and churned.

Finally he surfaced, then rolled over and quit,
I beached and unhooked him, he gasped and he spit.
I'd lost track of time, throughout our long fight,
Although I had won, would to kill him be right?
It didn't take long, to feel I was wrong, and a feeling of guilt festered in me,
With a tear in my eye, I bade him good bye, watching him swim away wild and free.

OREGON DEAR OREGON

Oh Oregon, Dear Oregon, you're eternal in my blood,
Forever are you in my heart and soul.
From your rocky coastal ramparts, to your valley's fertile mud,
Up and o'er the mountains, to where your wheat fields roll.

I've shaded 'neath your canopies, of virgin old growth stands,
Roamed your lonely deserts, and I've heard the coyotes howl.
I've combed your windy beaches, till my ears were numb from sand,
Plied your nameless canyons, where the bear and cougars prowl.

I've trod your lofty mountain tops, braved your endless snows,
Stood agape and breathless at the splendor of your fall.
I've been lashed by the Columbia, when the fierce gorge wind blows,
And heard the Bull Elk bugle his primeval mating call.

From your pristine lakes aplenty, teeming brim with fish,
To your boundless wilderness, so rich in fowl and game.
I've partaken of your bounty, you gratify my every wish,
Oh Oregon, dear Oregon, in my soul you've staked your claim.

A ROGUE AWAKENING

Holed up in a cabin on the banks of the Rogue,
I wrote verse and I pondered and sighed,
I was ambling through canyons, so rugged and steep,
as deep into the wilds I plied.

I could feel the stare, of someone not there,
as wearily onward I trod;
'Twas adventure I'd sought, but instead what I got,
was a glimpse of the wonders of God.

And Lord what a sight, in summers twilight,
watching bats try to chase down stars;
Those planes are so rude, how dare they intrude,
I wish they'd all fly off to Mars!

I never would care to bring grief to no bear,
that never did nothin' to me;
They rumble, tumble, fumble and stumble,
and race to the top of the honey tree.

High in the skies, what a treat for sore eyes,
like puppets on angels strings.
Bald eagles soar, above the din and the roar,
waving at us with their wings.

Held captive I stare, through the rivers glare,
at salmon cruising below.
These wonders won't cease, and offer such peace,
only one humbled can know.

Spiders make wings, from long silky strings,
bumming a ride from the breeze.
Each day I see, special ordered for me,
beauty that weakens my knees.

95

Those rocks on her banks, some bigger than tanks,
    worn smooth as a baby's butt.
From the great Crater Lake, she crawls like a snake,
    all the way to the sea she's cut.

Through oak groves galore, madrones by the score,
    through fir stands tall and great;
She's carved canyon walls, like cathedral halls,
    through miles of real estate.

Further I trekked, onward I pressed,
    crazed for the next mountain's crest.
Through silver grey snags, o'er mossy back crags,
    undaunted, I harried my quest.

Razor backed mountains, too many for countin',
    leap skyward, and stand in defiance.
I'm so far from home, and I'm so all alone,
    the solitude shatters the silence.

And once she's caught ya, she's always got ya,
    she'll lure you, and cause you to rave;
Was it happenstance? My river romance?
Who knows, but we're kith to the grave.

Taking a break from writing on the deck.

Hard at work on "Out of Oregon" at Paradise.

97

RIVER GUIDES

*This poem is dedicated to the hearty men and women who have heard
their calling to the wild and proudly answered it.*

O'er the savage rapids swift, in rafts and boats they glide,
Dauntless buccaneers of the rivers, cascading down the mountainside.
Fearless crusaders, white water invaders, the pirates of the west,
Tamers of the raging rivers wild, oarsman elite, the very best.
Lend unto us your wisdom, engage us with your down home wit,
Share with us your rivers lore, whilst 'round your fires we all sit.

Unto you our lives we trust, through canyons boulder strewn and deep,
'Neath a canopy of stars we lay, as babes in mangers, soft we sleep.
Take us where the eagles soar, show us where the osprey nest,
Make us one with the wilderness, we're so proud to be your guest.
Row us where the big ones lurk, cook them up for us to eat,
Enrich our lives through your work, in blazing sun or driving sleet.

Give us memories that we'll keep, for when were old and gray,
We'll relive the times we spent, on rivers wild and far away.
Blessed with patience near eternal, strong, robust, a kindred spirit,
Instill in us your love of nature, help us live it, make us hear it.
River Guides, Oh River Guides, keep pristine these wild places,
River Guides, Oh River Guides, may long you live, in God's good graces.

BALLOONS AIN'T FOR KIDS

A summer I will never forget was in the mid 1980's, up in the Cascade mountain range above the beautiful little town of Sweet Home, Oregon. It was on Gold Creek, a small tributary of Quartzville Creek, it was very rugged and beautiful country.

The yarder engineer and I lived in a 1950-something, single axle camp trailer on the banks of Quartzville Creek. The living conditions were spartan at best, but the ambience was unrivaled and remains with me to this day.

We shared our stretch of the river bank with a couple of retired guys who didn't seem to know much about retiring, they were up there gold mining. I'm not talking about a placer mine either, they were hard rock mining with powder and heavy equipment. Carl and Sam, were their names, if memory serves me correct. They were pretty well off I gathered from all of the equipment they were running, their claim was a patented claim, and they would take off some timber from time to time.

I'll always treasure those nights that we sat around the camp fire passing the jug around. When we ran out of stories and lies to tell, we would just listen to the night sounds and the creek. It was one of those nights after everyone had passed out and went on to bed that I had the fire and the night to myself and 20 some years later inspired me to write, "Camp Fire Journeys".

I was working for Flying Scotsman Inc., this was a balloon side and turned out to be every bit the adventure I had hoped for … and then some! Balloon logging is a very expensive and dangerous method of getting logs out. It's usually used on very steep ground, that has sensitive environmental issues, things can go bad very quickly and be costly and sometimes fatal.

When a conventional tower lands a turn of logs, a man runs out and unbells the chokers and the rigging is sent back out to the brush. If you have "tight uns" (which you always will) you can kick 'em, roll 'em,

99

whatever you need to do via hand signals to the engineer; no big deal for a good chaser.

Enter balloons, when a balloon lands a turn of logs, the chaser has to hide under the landing yarder to avoid being hit by all the debris falling out of the sky from the turn. If he survives that, then he can work on getting the chokers unbelled. The yarder engineer literally had to "land" the logs. He pulls 'em right out of the sky, damndest thing you ever saw!

The Chaser's job is hard and dangerous. When the logs touch down, they don't stay still for very long as the balloon is always bobbing around and so are the logs; You watch your tago line when it gets some slack in it, then you go in and unbell the chokers. When it starts back up, you get out and wait for slack again, to get the rest of your chokers undone. Invariably under pressure for production, a man will push his luck from time to time. This is usually when fate will send you little warnings that you aren't superman and to slow down a little … or else. I was to get such a warning one sunny summer day.

The rigging crew had been cutting a fat hog in the ass all day long and the landing was in shambles. I was a pretty good chaser, but still pretty green to balloon logging. When the balloon takes the rigging up and back out to the brush is when the fun starts on the landing. The chaser must limb the logs, buck any and all broken ends, brand each log, both ends and then bunch them all up with a grapple skidder and run them 1/4 mile down the road to a "safe" landing where the trucks are loaded out and sent to town.

That's a lot of work for one man! I had logs scattered from hell to breakfast, and losing ground every turn.

The crew was being paid a visit this afternoon by the owner, Mr. Faye Stewart. We were advised to have a lot of wood on the landing and have our side "looking good and puttin out wood", and by God we were gonna see to it. Aside from having logs all up and down the road and over the bank, the landing chute wasn't far from being completely plugged, that means everything stops. Mr. Stewart would not be a happy camper to see his whole crew standing around looking stupid while he's paying 'em for it! That would be unacceptable, why, we'd sooner have a sister in a whorehouse than have the owner find us screwed to a stand-still!

The yarder engineer told the rigging crew to slack off a bit so I could get caught up. I was having to climb up twelve feet or more to unbell the chokers, to make matters worse the wind always picks up in the afternoon and today was no exception. We never had a precise time of arrival for Mr. Stewart, so we pretty much had to be ready for him all the time.

By mid afternoon the wind was picking up pretty good and we were having quite a time of it on the landing, being right on top of a ridge like we were. They didn't have it near as bad out in the brush, as they were a ways below us in a canyon. As soon as the ship is below the ridge, the rigging smoothed right out.

About an hour and a half before quittin' time we hear the chopper inbound, and it's show time. We had just landed a turn, and I was putting some chokers from the last turn on the tago line to send them back out. I glanced over at the chopper touching down. Half blinded from the dust, somehow the tago line and chokers whipped around my backside, then dropped and came back up, I think that's what happened, I'll never really know. When the line goes back up it has a hold of my leg, and is shaking me around like a rug on the landing. I remember looking at the chopper and seeing Mr. Stewart watching my antics with his hands cupped to his face in astonishment!

Then it turned me loose, just as fast as it had snared me, bam ... just like that, it was over. I was laying on the ground, I couldn't see any blood, my leg hurt a little but nothing major. I slowly stood up, walked around a bit, stretched a little, how 'bout them apples; I was sore but otherwise unscathed.

By now Mr. Stewart's chopper has landed, I'm somewhat shaken still, mad as hell and getting madder. I looked over at the chopper and there is Mr. Stewart summoning me over with his index finger to talk to him.

I'm thinking to myself, if he says one smart ass thing to me I'm gonna chew his ass up one side down the other, repeat it once, then quit and go to town and start a tab at the Skyline Inn.

With chip on shoulder I strode over to see what Mr. Stewart wanted. When I got there he says to me, "young man, do you know how much it would cost me if you got killed up here?"

That was it, this ole boy was gonna get both barrels, and then I was headin' for town.

Just as I was getting ready to tell him off, I see the yarder engineer, my roommate, and esteemed beer swilling colleague of many years warding me off, with a clenched fist no less. I can still see his lips moving, saying, "don't do it, don't you do it kid". After considering his size and passion for fighting, I was inclined to agree with him.

I looked at Mr. Stewart and apologized for alarming him and told him not to worry, we do this all the time, then went right ahead on 'er!!

Mr. Stewart carried on with his 'tour 'de operationes' and was soon back aboard his helicopter and off into the wild blue yonder.

I stayed on for a few more weeks, but after a few more pretty close calls I figured I'd had enough of this shit, and I went and found me a skidder and some nice flat ground to run it on.

I found out later that the same balloon was owned by another man I worked for. Pat Solderberg, he used it up in Alaska.

I don't think they use balloons to much any more, they're too expensive and dangerous. You've really got to watch out for yourself around a balloon. Balloon logging in storms is a no no, especially a thunder storm!

They can be real hoot in the snow and rain when they get heavy and tip to unload. Chunks of snow and ice could kill you if they hit you, and I've had many a shower from a balloon! I've stood next to the landing yarder in a good wind and seen the front end hopping up and down.

The engineer would have to slack 'er off on occasion and set 'er back on the ground, I learned real quick not to set saws and lunches any where close to the Ol' girl.

I'VE GOT TO GO BACK

I've got to go back to the tall timber soon,
Back where the big firs sawtooth the sky;
Back where I rise to the cries of a loon,
Back where the osprey, and eagles still fly.
The city and its woes, scare me to death,
The squalor and stench burns in my eyes.
My heart is pounding, I can't catch my breath,
To tell you the truth, I'm sick of the lies.

The bells and whistles, the honking of horns,
The screech of tires, the curse and the yell.
I need to wake up to clear, quiet morns,
To be stuck in this city's, like living in hell.
I'm gagging on a swill, mistaken for air,
And I can't trust a soul that I see.
I'd just as soon lay in a rattlesnakes lair,
I can't stay in the city, I need to be free.

I need to have my campfire at night,
I've got to be able to count my stars.
I'm blinded by the glare of the city's light,
And froze like a deer, in the eyes of their cars.
I've got to get back, amid valley and peak,
I need a good lashing from the wind and rain.
I need the culture of a babbling creek,
I've got to get back to my mountains again.

I've not seen a smile since I looked in the mirror,
Their furrowed, gaunt faces tell of their fears.
They scurry like mice, amid the din and furor,
And they've all got cell phones stuck in their ears.
I gave it my best,
I failed your test,
I need some rest.
I need a good lashing from the wind and rain,
I've got to get back to my mountains again.

ROGUE RIVER RASCAL

I was feelin' mighty tired, close to bein' expired,
So I lay myself down in the shade of a tree.
I was soon fast asleep, in peaceful slumber deep,
When all of a sudden like, a voice yelled down at me:

"I'm the Rogue River Rascal,
Just in case you haven't heard,
I felt it only fair that you should know.
I'm the Rogue River Rascal,
And you ought to pass the word,
I'm the roughest bull there is in the rodeo.
I got a porcupine for a milkin' stool,
I got a real live coonskin hat.
I use Crater Lake for my swimmin' pool,
I got a four eyed ring-tailed cat".

"I got a buffalo robe for my sleepin' sack,
I use a beaver tail for swattin' flies.
I was sent to Hell but fought my way back,
I told Hathaway Jones most his lies.
I keep my britches up with a cougar's tail,
I went over Rainey in a hollerd out log.
I whupped up on a bear 'till I made him wail,
And a Timber Wolf thinks he's my dog".

"I'm the Rogue River Rascal,
And I play in the cold hard rains,
It's the only time I ever wash my clothes.
I'm the Rogue River Rascal,
And though my legacy remains,
Where I'll wind up next, nobody knows.
There's a Bald Eagle sittin' on my shoulder,
A black bear cub eatin' out of my hand.
I sleep like a baby from atop a big boulder,
When I hit town, they strike up the band".

"Illahee Annie, was the love of my life,
But she was homely as an old basset hound.
But I took her anyhow, and made her my wife,

But she jumped from a limb into the river and drowned.
I've told Zane Grey a story or two,
I've rubbed elbows 'till they both was sore.
I drank with the Generals, till the bottle was through,
Left the whole damn bunch passed out on the floor.

"I led Sheriff Boice on a wild goose chase,
Then pulled him off the rocks, a couple weeks later.
We laughed like hell, and he closed the case,
He wasn't bein' nice, just a good Neighbor.
I'm scared of your cities, despise your cars,
And I loathe your concrete paths.
I'll spend my days beneath these stars,
My fate's at the mercy of nature's wrath".

"I've clung to cliffs like a mountain goat,
Howled at the moon till I lost my voice.
I taught Glen Wooldridge how to row his boat,
I know the Rogue River as well as Court Boice.
I don't cuss in church, or try to be rude,
Daddy was a Mormon, they call me the Jack.
I'm not real polished and a tad bit crude,
I'm the Rogue River Rascal, and that's a fact".

"I've pitched thunder eggs to Bobby Doerr,
Taught Ernie and Casey both how to fish.
I've been around the horn and back for more,
Just to see Mother Nature, my Rogue River Dish.
I've toiled on the bar, with a pan 'tween my knees,
Shivered like a leaf, from the placer's cold.
I worked shoulder to shoulder with the hoards of Chinese
I saw brother pit brother, agin sacks of gold".

"I've seen thunder heads spit lightning bolts,
Felt the roar echo through canyons deep.
I've broke wild elk like mustang colts,
Roused the dead from their eternal sleep.
I've been bushwhacked, and left for dead,
Hog jawed more than I can recall.
Make sure you're right, then go right ahead
You see: there's a little of the Rascal, livin' in us all".

Court Boice, owner of Paradise Lodge with author at Paradise.

Author with Steam Donkey, Reedsport, Oregon.

ROGUE RIVER NIGHTS

I bared my soul to the wild, wide eyed like a child,
As I bask in the hue of a harvest moon.
I was taken back by it all, 'neath the timber so tall,
There were shadows at midnight, just like at noon.

Then who should appear, but Daisy the deer,
She grazed, then lay down by my side.
We sat there together, aware of each other,
Each knew the other had nothing to hide.

As on cue they were there, old Blacky the bear,
Pepé the skunk, and Rocky the coon.
The crickets and frogs, hopped up on their logs,
Chimed in with the river and sang me a tune.

There were a million stars, Venus and Mars,
Critters that go bump in the night.
All of our eyes, were glued to the skies,
Hard to imagine a more beautiful sight.

Then up came a breeze, it danced in the trees,
Woke up the fire, that had dozed off to sleep.
The smoke waft slow, it hung ever so low,
A wisp in the canyon, where the river runs deep.

The bank says I'm bust, but it's in God that I trust,
And in these wilds, where no man has lease.
I'm happy and content, my time is well spent,
I don't pay a dime for this splendor and peace.
And just where do I fall, in the scheme of it all,
I must have a place, 'cause I'm here.
I forsake the rat race, for this heavenly place,
And a life in the wilds with nothing to fear.

107

The Shooting and Cremation of Pepé le Pew
(With apologies to Robert Service)

This story I'm a tellin', 'bout that skunk we was smellin',
I swear to you folks is true.
He was a little pole cat, he sprayed this and that,
We called the little stinker 'Pepé le Pew'.

Now the skipper Court, was a jolly good sport,
But he'd taken all of Pepé that he could.
Pepé's scent we couldn't mask, so Court gave me the task,
To rid the lodge of Pepé boy for good.

With great care I laid my traps, in hopes of that perhaps,
I'd catch our little uninvited guest.
But every night he'd spray, and he wouldn't go away,
He'd grown to be a rotten little pest.

I finally caught the little fart, but I found I lacked the heart,
To shoot my little cute, but smelly foe.
So the skipper took the gun, and though it weren't no fun,
He did the job, but then he had to go.

We finally had our skunk, but Lordy how he stunk,
And our guests, were just arousing from their sleep.
I had a little hunch, I was gonna lose my lunch,
Disposing of the stinkin' little creep.

And there we were at last, his stinkin' days had passed,
But I couldn't help but feel somewhat sad.
I choked and gagged like I'd been gassed,
What a shame the little bugger smelled so bad.

THE FEVER

I've read the verse that Service wrote, of the trail of '98,
Of the biting cold and solitude, and the 'funny ways of fate'.
Days and nights unending, spent in dark, and death like cold,
Men like demons scheming, for the chance to die for gold.
They lay the earth wide open, they were savage in their lust,
From sea to sea the cry rang out, "'tis the Klondike, boys or bust".

Wife and child abandoned, crops withered, homes were lost,
They sold their souls to the Devil, 'twas the Yukon, damn the cost.
Their beasts were burdened woefully, and lashed on until they fell,
The weak were culled out one by one, and the rest marched onto Hell.
The Chiltkoot Pass was a human chain, from its base clean o'er its top,
Their greed drove them blindly on, no man would dare to stop.

The trail turned to a frothing foam, wrought with danger, start to end,
The thunderous roar of rapids echoed 'round each river bend.
Their rafts were smashed and splintered in canyons swift and wild,
Then spit them out on the river bank, and they whimpered there like a child.
Yet on they pressed, like men possessed, with a lust no man could hide,
Gold was all they cared about, by no laws would they abide.

The first ones there got their gold, they took more than their share,
But gold's no good in the wilderness, so they sought the cities glare.
They hit the skidrows eagerly, with their pokes chock full of dust,
Every man was your friend back then, yet no man dare you trust.
The con men were thick as fleas, jaded harlots all in a row,
Like buzzards on the prowl they wait, for the hapless sourdough.

But they know the day is soon to come, when the poke is gone at last,
They'll wake up in the ditch one morning and can't recall the past.
Then back out on the pike again, back into the snow and cold,
Back into the frozen Arctic zone, gold crazed, brazen, and bold.
Their quest for the gold will never end, not 'till the day they die,
With a pick and shovel in their hand, and a gleam of yellow in their eye.

THE CRASH

This little incident occurred in the late 1980's, up in the coast range of Oregon in the Siuslaw National Forest, I believe. We were tower logging with an old home made yarder. It was a Hienz 57, mix kind of a critter. It was self propelled, by means of a 1950's something vintage army tank. Which of course, had the turret removed and replaced by a hoist, or a set of drums if you prefer, two yarding drums and a haywire drum. She had a home made square steel spar about 40' or 50' high and was guyed with 6 guy lines. The old bastard didn't look to good, but actually it wasn't a bad little yarder, though it did have its drawbacks.

There was no cab, just a shed roof, sort of like the old steam donkeys used to have. There were no air controls on this old girl either. It was all manual control levers and foot brakes. When the operator got to sit down, (which wasn't very often), his perch was an old steel tractor seat. If the operator wasn't careful, he could get bucked off of 'er pretty damned easy.

It had two Diesel engines, one for the carrier and another one for the yarder. You couldn't tell which one was the loudest, or smoked the worst. The tank part, or the carrier, was steered by pulling on two levers. You pull on the left lever, she turns left, and vice versa. Before the old girl would steer and stop properly, one had to drive it forwards while pulling on both steering levers. The purpose of this was to dry off the brakes, as they would be moist from the condensation of the previous night.

We had finished up one setting and moved the yarder to the next landing, which was about a half mile away. When we got it to the next setting, we set about notching a few guy line stumps and packed a few sections out in the brush for the lay out. Being rather late in the day, we never got around to rigging her up, so we left her there for the night and would finish rigging up in the morning. Right now it was Miller time!

Upon our arrival the next morning, we all set about our various

110

tasks involved in rigging up the yarder. Woodrow, the hooktender, went out in the brush to string out the haywire we had packed out the day before. Old Bill was finishing up notching the guy line stumps and Yours Truly was putting the final touches on the landing site with the Cat. The owner was back at the last landing, loading out the first string of trucks. He would bring the shovel over and join us when he was done.

Having finished up with the landing, the yarder engineer, we called him "Durwood," figured it was time to move the old girl into place and raise the spar so we could get 'er rigged up and go to logging. Durwood started it up and warmed 'er up a bit and then began to move it into its new home. However, amid all the hub bub of the rig up he forgot to dry off the brakes! As he pulled it into its setting, he pulled on the brakes to stop but she didn't stop. He was right on the edge of the landing when he applied the brakes, and that was all she wrote.

Seeing his impending demise, Durwood did the only thing he could do, and that is abandon ship.

He made it out just in time too. I was just getting off the cat and I looked over to see if Durwood had the yarder in place, I couldn't believe my eyes when I saw Durwood sprawled out on the ground and the ass end of the old dinosaur going over the edge, and down in the hole.

This really shook me up. It was very hot and dry out there and the fire danger was high and this could very easily turn out to be a catastrophe in the making.

I ran over and checked on Durwood. He was bruised and shaken up, but not really hurt. I ran over to the edge of the landing and about 100 feet or so down the hill there she was. Smoking like a house afire, laying on her side and still running, her tracks gnashing about like some giant wounded animal going through its death throes.

By now, Woodrow had heard all the commotion. He had made his way to the scene from down below and was trying to get her shut down. Bill finally made it over and I dispatched him down with a couple of fire extinguishers and shovels. I headed for the crummy, to drive over and get the owner and the radio in case we had to get some fire crews up there. I jumped in the crummy and someone had left a window down, the whole interior was covered with old growth horse flies! There were hundreds, if not thousands of them, and the little bastards swarmed me and started biting the shit out of me! There was nothing I could do except keep going, as I had to get the owner over there and on the double.

He knew something was amiss when he saw how fast I was going. When I got to his landing I jumped out of the crummy and I forgot to put it in gear. It took off headed for the log deck. That crummy was our only mode of transportation, if we lost it we would be up the creek especially if we had to get out of there in a hurry. Throwing caution to the wind, I ran as fast as I could and finally caught up to it about 5 feet before it was going to hit the log deck and got 'er stopped. Having averted that disaster, the owner and I then headed for the real disaster. Woodrow had gotten it shut off and unhooked the batteries before the engine seized up and they had dug a fire line around it, all the smoke was from oil on the exhaust. We had dodged the proverbial bullet as far as a fire was concerned. I'm not sure just how, but we did. The owner kept Bill up there to fire watch while he loaded out logs and sent the rest of us home. We would be off for about 6 weeks until it got fished up and repaired. The owner had insurance on it, but as with most logging equipment insurance, he had a $10,000 deductible, he had to fork out first.

Durwood was real upset, and he had every right to be. The poor bastard started bawling on the way home, but what's done is done— weren't nothin' a few six pacs wouldn't take care of!

THE BONNY DUST

Since the dawn of man, have tales been told,
Of the fervent quest for the bonny dust.
They lied, cheated, and killed for the gold,
They were blind with fever, and mad in their lust.

They scoured the rivers and scaled the peaks,
They thawed the tundra and blasted the pit.
Miserable days, became torturous weeks,
Visions of riches, would not let them quit.

Partners and foes, through times hard and lean,
A helping hand up, or a knife at the throat.
A windlass to turn, or a sluice box to clean,
A mine gone bust, or bonanza to gloat.

Hydraulic monitors chewed away slopes,
Mighty gold dredges tore up the rivers.
Broken men living on beans and high hopes,
Moonshine hooch eats at their livers.

They prayed for big nuggets, in all of the streams,
Pay dirt was always one shovel away.
But the fortunes they won, were only in dreams,
For men with the fever, there's no other way.

Before they know it, they're old, gray, and bent,
Grub is still low, and as usual they're broke.
Two days in town, and their moneys all spent,
Sprawled in the ditch, with no dust in their poke.

But the wilds are a calling, and the claim is still there,
With spirits renewed, he's up for the hike.
The sluice boxes are full, but the cupboard is bare,
It's a matter of time, 'till he hits the big strike.

Big fortunes were made, and most of them lost,
There was no one to hear all the tales they told.
But most never thought of or tallied the cost,
Or what they would give to never find gold.

Hecera Head, Florence, Or.

114

THE OCEAN

Roll on, roll on, Oh mighty Pacific,
You're waves eternally pounding ashore.
With might unchallenged, and fury horrific,
Fool hardy mariners resting on your floor.

The moon, from heaven meters the tides,
Celestial clockwork, endless its quest.
Primeval swill from whence life abides,
Saltwater abyss where man is a guest.

Stoic stone sentries jut from her beaches,
Sand and time, will erode them away.
Shells litter the shore and a starfish reaches,
For sand dollars that fall where they may.

No words can portray, how she swallows the sun,
To put an end to another day.
Mirroring the stars when day's light is done,
Whimsical mentor, moon beaming away.

White clad light houses reach for the sky,
From their perches among the cliffs.
From out of the fog, hear mariners cry,
Long lost at sea, adrift in their skiffs.

She's calm as a pond, then catches a wind,
And whips herself into a fit.
When wise men wonder, where all things begin,
Alone on her beaches they sit.

For centuries untold, tales unfold,
Of those who would try and tame her.
Never ending wonders to behold,
Things are never the same here.

She's scantily clad, so ever alluring,
She's mother to all that we know.
She's everlasting and all enduring,
Wildly dancing when the winds blow.

WESTERN SKIES

Western skies, so clear and bright,
Just as lovely now, as way back then.
Please cast my way your stars tonight,
I'll try and count them all again.

Have them bring some coyotes along,
I'm so lonesome, can't you see?
Have them sing their timeless song,
And keep me company.

I'll day dream 'mid gentle breezes,
That softly whisper unto me.
My restless soul, your mood appeases,
And my heart, you've set it free

No time for slumber in morning dew,
The new day arrives, with a chill.
Can't wait to spend the day with you,
We'll tap the clouds and drink our fill.

I'll chase you miles today to earn my keep,
Should I tire, would you wait?
We'll roam the prairie grasses deep,
Stalk through forests tall and great.

A canyon beckons, I hear mountains call,
How good you are to me;
Oh God, how I love it, can I have it all,
Priceless treasures, all for free?

Lakes shimmer below, like diamonds in dirt,
The glare is hurting my eyes.
I'll stay here always, what could it hurt,
To live my life 'neath western skies.

SUMMER NIGHTS

Have you ever laid back and gazed up at the skies,
And caught a glimpse of a shooting star?
Saw a moon so bright that it hurt your eyes,
As it lit up the night from the heavens afar.

Watching silver tipped clouds flirt with the trees,
While their boughs try to shoo them away.
Their perfume lingers on the evening breeze,
Hear the trees as they creak and sway.

An owl queries "who", from out of the woods,
And a coyote answers him back.
Take respite, from pursuit of material goods,
It's peace of mind, not money we lack.

The bats and the bugs, wage their timeless war,
That neither can ever win.
Marching waves lapping at shore,
Tease you to sleep with a grin.

Summer smells and wishing wells
And innocence only a child could know.
And days gone past, like magic spells,
Come back to mind from long ago.

Thunder claps and lightning bolts,
God sent wonders from heaven above.
Strikes the Earth with a mighty jolt,
Be safe in the arms of the one you love.

SEASONS

Seasons ever changing, time keeps marching on,
Ebb and flow, life and death, some things never change.
One season dawns anew, another one is gone,
Taken all for granted, unpredictable and strange.

The sum of seasons totaled, tallies up to be the year,
Spring time is the season of new birth.
Snow and ice abated, buds and blossoms soon appear,
All enthralled, elated, by the bounty of the Earth.

Summer time rejuvenates, turns muddy paths to dust,
The Sun's like a ball of orange in a hazy sky.
Summer gives us time to do, the things we must,
Get our house in order 'fore the snow begins to fly.

Summer lingers on, but alas, succumbs to fall,
Seasons come and go and always will.
Clouds ominous appear and the wind is prone to squall,
Dog days of summer time give way to the chill.

Autumn colors bright, render mountain sides ablaze,
Frost on the pumpkin early in the morn.
The harvest moon is high, and shorter wane the days,
Coyotes howl echoes, ancient and forlorn.

Old Man Winter's here, a knockin' on our doors,
Make ready sled and sleigh, go for a ride;
Shovel roof and sidewalk, never ending chores,
Head for the frozen pond, run skate and slide.

MORE GRAB ASS

Even my earliest recollections are salted with a propensity for practical jokes, or in the loggers vernacular, "grab ass". Harmless for the most part, usually amusing, although embarrassing and annoying to the victim of the moment, grab assing, is seen by a lot of loggers as a necessary 'vent' that helps them deal with the dangers and rigors of their occupation.

The oft maligned "crummy", has been the stage for many a prankster down through the years, including yours truly. The opportunities are limited only by the imagination and run the gamut from the time honored silent beer fart, to elaborately choreographed affairs. Here's a few I got a kick out of the most.

This I shouldn't have done, but I didn't have the where with all to restrain myself. A shovel operator we called Grunt, would bear the brunt of my mischievous stunt. It was in the winter and we were logging a unit up near the top of the Santiam Pass, Scott Cr. I believe it was. We were leaving Sweet Home at O dark thirty in the morning, the commute took three hours each way when the weather was really bad. This afforded the crew to get a little more shut eye in route to the job. Old Grunt had a real nice little set up. He had the very back bench seat in the Chevy Suburban that served as our crummy. He had himself a blanket and pillow, the boss man even had a heater put in it for him, old Grunt slept like baby.

Due to snow the road in some places had gotten pretty bad. One particular spot had developed a large speed bump, or mogul if you prefer, that prompted ODOT to erect a sign warning motorists to slow down for it.

Wide Open Olsen was our usual crummy driver. He had stayed at the office a little too late the night before so I was filling in for him, as he would nod off at the wheel while he was driving.

The crew was sleeping peacefully with me at the helm as we ap-

119

proached the now infamous mogul, worthy of its own warning sign. In a flash of brilliance, I got an idea for another prank. I'd hit the mogul a little too fast and wake the boys up, I figured I'd get a laugh or two out of that.

The bastards damn near killed me. I was probably doing 20 mph, maybe a shade faster when we hit that thing, and boy did the shit hit the fan.

I made sure to have my eye on mirror when we hit so's I could see the action, especially Grunt, the poor s.o.b. When the back wheels hit, he flew up and hit the ceiling like he'd come off a buckin' bull and came down in heap on the floor in front of his bed. Pretty much the same thing happened to everybody except me. I was ready for it, all the tools and lunches and thermoses went crashing around. As it turns out, my prank was rather ill advised, I quickly saw my salvation in saying, "I must have dosed off", and it was just coincidence that it happened where it did. I held to my guns and stuck with my lie. Eventually the grumbling eased off and all was forgiven, but I'd wager not forgotten!

Another one guaranteed to raise the roof, is the venerable "torch". You've got to be sneaky to pull it off, it is best if you are in the back seat to do this one. Tradition has long held that loggers cut out the hem of their pants, (stagged off pants) to aid in their escape by tearing, should they be snagged by a limb or something. This leaves a ragged fringe around the would be cuffs of a logger's pants, it's been like that from the start, and remains true to this day.

From my roost in back seat, I would slink silently to the floor boards, and like the snake I was, I'd slither under the seat in front of me, and I would light their cuffs with my bic lighter, I could usually get three or four of them going before they woke up to the flames and smoke!

I can remember it like it was yesterday, I used to have the whole crummy in stitches doing that, even the ones I set on fire. We've had to pull over and get it out of our system, it's even more of riot if we're drunk!

A gag I got a lot of mileage out of over the years was one that I played on not fellow loggers, but on hapless wannabes.

A few of us would head into a watering hole, and begin to do what we do best, drinking beer and swapping lies. After a while there is usually some young buck in wings who sees what fun and camaraderie those loggers have and inquires if we might need some help, as he buys us a pitcher of beer. We gratefully accept his beer offering, and begin to question him.

"Do you have what it takes to be a logger?" we'd ask, "what about the danger, and long hours, can you stand the weather?" On the questioning goes, he gives us all the right answers, just the way we did at one time. We tell him we must have more beer, and deliberate amongst ourselves to discuss the matter.

After our deliberation we motioned our young protege over for a few more questions, then we finally tell him we are going to give him a try. The kid is always elated and more often than not, he was good for a few more beers. Upon adjourning for the night, we tell our victim to be at such and such place at 4:30 a.m., and don't be late. We tell them to be sure and have a lunch, boots and gloves to be ready to hit 'er hard, and he assures us he'll be there. The punch line of course is that we never show up!

By some small miracle, I've never met up with any of them and had to come clean!

THE FALL

Summer's been spent, it just up and went,
It does it every year.
Nights get colder, the moon grows bolder,
Skies have never been so clear.

The breeze shakes trees of their painted leaves,
And lays a carpet o'er the ground.
In the call of geese, hear the solemn peace,
Of an ancient, far off, lonely sound.

The woods are ablaze, in a rainbow maze,
Of yellows, green, and red.
The critters are a dash to tithe their cache,
Making ready for days ahead.

Clouds are coming, thunder's a drumming,
Looks like rain is on the way.
A sky once blue, has changed its hue,
To an almost eerie, ashen gray .

There's leaves to rake, loaves to bake,
Hordes of pumpkins in the patch.
There's wood to chop, hogs to slop,
Colds for all the kids to catch.

The Fall means turkey, venison jerky,
Maybe a bowel of stew or two.
There's fireside talks, moonlit walks,
Blue smoke curling from the wood stove flue.

There's colors galore, they scream and roar,
They shout from every crevasse of earth.
Fall lends one to ponder, to dream and wonder,
To think about life, and what it's worth.

It's the season of reflection, of ambition and direction,
Of testing your mettle and proving your lot.
Of loving and living, of sharing and forgiving,
Of being grateful for what you've got.

HONKERS

Every fall, the cold winds blow down,
Their bounty from the north.
They fill the skies high over town,
As they see-saw back and forth.

They rest on wings, a mile high,
As they make their way down south.
Announcing themselves from the sky,
By honking word of mouth.

With fields found, they funnel down,
Set their wings and meet the ground.
They turn green fields muddy brown,
Alert for hunter and his hound.

They know the cold, they know their way,
They mate for life it's said;
How many pairs must one slay,
For a soft down pillow under head?

Their lonesome call tells us all,
That winter's almost here.
Honker hunters crave the Fall,
Memories made, held fond and dear.

THE YEAR

Winter's grip has begun to slip, there's a mood swing in the air,
Birds and bees come alive in the trees, and lakes lose their icy glare.

A field and stream, a long winter's dream, spring has finally sprung,
All things sing the songs of spring, that winter left unsung.

Appetites defeated, by the long winter meted, out of slumber arisen,
Furred and feathered, free and untethered, revel in all that's given.

Famine or feast, goes the way of the beast, complacent, unable to wonder,
The sun's warm rays, usher in dog days, and the earth's a pantry to plunder.

Riding high, in a Summer sky shining down upon on all God made,
A sun so bright, a blinding light, a day's well spent asleep in the shade.

The longest day, has past away, and now comes a nip in the wind,
Summertime's past, too good to last, make haste, let the fall begin.

O', how lovely the call, of each new fall, with hillsides all ablaze,
With quickened steps, like a promise unkept, I seek out the wilds like one who's crazed.

In crimson and gold, the trees unfold, and shed leaves o'er the forest floor,
The sound of geese, fill one with peace, and soothe the urge to settle a score.

The year has past, but it's here at last, Old Man Winter hits with surprise,
The wind will blow, and the cold you'll know, and white that'll sear your eyes.

Them prepared best, take time to rest, seek out solace in the sound of rain,
Let your soul unwind, as you seek to find, the strength to do it again.

RISE TO THE CALL

The deeds done that morn, by those cowards we scorn,
On Tuesday, Eleven, September.
Will haunt mankind for all of time,
And forever be a day to remember.

We just can't equate, their zeal for hate,
Yet, towards that evil end they trod.
They've spat in the face, of the human race,
And done it in the name of God.

Dare they stop to think, they pray we'll blink,
Because they've ran out of places to run.
They claim it's an honor to die, we'll ask not why,
But we'll damn sure see it gets done.

As the smoke is clearing, our unity's endearing,
As always we rise to the call.
As they run for their holes, and pray for their souls,
The writing is etched on their wall.

There was Valley Forge, with forefather George,
And by George, we'll do it again.
Our Civil War, pit kin agin kin,
From out of the rubble, rose united men.

In World War One, we crushed the Hun,
Freed the world, from the grips of war.
In World War Two, we fought two fronts at once,
Led the fight for freedom once more.

In '53, it was Korea you see,
And that barely seemed to faze us.
Then 'Nam came along, and right or wrong,
Americans awed and amazed us.

There was Desert Shield and Desert Storm,
Then that mess in Kosovo;
Around the world, Old Glory unfurled,
To freedom, she won't say no.

The line has been crossed, so much has been lost,
It will never again be the same.
What a dastardly deed we were done,
Low down, dog dirty, and lame.

CRITTERS

All God's critters, to me, is special things,
They fly and swim, they slither and crawl.
They got horns and tails, and some got wings,
They're fat and skinny and they're short and tall.

I've seen them in deserts, forests and farms,
I've seen them in the oceans, rivers and in streams.
They're furred and feathered, and monkeys got arms
And I wonder if critters have hopes and dreams.

There's mommies and daddies and little ones too,
I've seen 'em all frolic in the spring.
There's bears that growl, and doves that coo,
And all them birdies, that chirp and sing.

There's critters so small, you can't even see 'em,
There's critters all over, everywhere you look.
There's prehistoric critters, down in the museum,
There's enough critters to fill a big book.

There's critters for day, and there's critters for night,
They've got critters for this, and there's one for that.
There's critters that hiss, that sting, and bite,
And nothing can flutter in the sky like a bat.

There's Mother Goose and my other goose,
And Daffy Ducks afloat on the lakes.
Way up in the north, there's Bullwinkle the moose,
And jungles and swamps are full of big snakes.

Critters give comfort to mens troubled souls,
Warmth and shelter, from life's stormy seas.
We can't let the critters keep paying the tolls,
While run amok humans do like they please.

127

OLD GROWTH GUS

Way off yonder, where the timber grows tall,
There toils a simple man, who's a tough ole cuss.
He craves the wild and solitude, and loggin' is his call,
Everybody knew him as 'Old Growth Gus.'

His home was a shanty, on a mountain side steep,
He shared with his pet, a skunk named Skeeter.
He'd rather log than eat, fish, or sleep,
He chewed a little bit, drank beer by the liter.

Now Old Gus was a hermit, been a loner all his life,
But it seemed to suit him, and he liked it alright.
But lately he'd been thinkin', 'bout catchin' him a wife,
So he headed into town, on a dark and stormy night.

The wind was a howlin' and the rain pourin' down,
When he fired up the cat and headed down the hill;
It took him two days, but he finally got to town,
With a mission on his mind, and no time to kill.

He dusted off his duds, and scrapped the jaggers off his mug,
Then set off to find himself a waterin' hole.
He cased out the skidrows, then got himself a jug,
Then he began to looking for that unsuspecting soul.

And there in the corner, passed out in her chair,
With her lunch in her lap, and her teeth in her hand;
She weren't much to look at, but Gus didn't care,
So off he went to get his love a wedding band.

There was no doubt about it, 'twas love at first sight,
And no truer love, has there ever been;
He was hoping she'd go easy, and not put up a fight,
And maybe even shave the whiskers off her chin.

They were married at the mill, on the outskirts of town,
And had their reception down at the riggin' shack;
She was a sight to behold, in her burlap wedding gown,
Ole Gus had to help her shave the hair off her back.

THE RUNAWAY

My first real job in the woods was with my buddy we'll call Lonnie, not counting the time I lied my way onto a skidder, and nearly wiped out the whole outfit.

Lonnie and I had been cutting firewood together and as usual I was coming up on the short end of the stick more often than not. After a brief executive meeting with the Old Lady, I tendered my resignation to Lonnie and went to work in a finish mill in Springfield, OR. It was pretty easy, and had a roof over it. It paid a whopping $4.50 an hour, a pretty fair wage for a mill rat back then.

Lonnie ended up working for the mill that we were selling our bigger diameter, 8-10' logs to.

He started out running a skidder, eventually wound up as the shovel operator, and the guy in charge when the boss was gone; which was most of the time.

One evening I was outside hard at work at one of my favorite past times, trying to fix my truck. Then lo and behold, up drives Lonnie old buddy. Lonnie says he wants me to come and work with him on this logging job, after a six pac or three, he's got me thinking that's a pretty damn good idea. I am to be the chaser, the chaser is the landing man. His job is to unbell the chokers as the machines bring logs in, then cut off any limbs remaining on them, buck broken ends, and then brand and paint the logs.

This was a pretty small outfit, it had a Clark 666 Ranger rubber tired skidder and a Case cat with a logging arch. It was about the size of a D5 Cat. These machines hauled the logs from the woods where they were cut to the landing. From there Lonnie loaded them out on log trucks with the mills brand spankin' new United log Loader, that was mounted on a '60 something Mack truck with the old over and under transmissions. Those were pretty tough for a novice like myself, but I'd be alright after a bit, I've always took well to equipment.

Lonnie arrived to pick me up at 5:00 a.m. sharp the next morning and off we go, headed for the job, a place just outside of Lebanon, OR.

130

called Lacomb. As we turned off of the paved road onto gravel, Lonnie ole buddy brings to light a minor glitch we could encounter. It seems that the owner is unaware of the fact that he has a new chaser! Knowing Lonnie, this doesn't really surprise me, so I just play it by ear and give it my best shot. Everything on the run, "ass holes and elbows", as we called it in the Marine Corps.

After a few days the owner gave me the nod, and put me on the payroll at $6.10 an hr. I was elated and promptly secured myself a regulation logger's suit; Hickory shirt, red suspenders, caulk boots, tin hat, the whole Mary Ann. I proudly wore my new uniform of the 'woods warrior', and in my youth felt almost invincible. After a few weeks, the not so glamorous side of logging rears its ugly head. I start learning about squeak heel, choker bells to the chins, and mud, lots of mud, knee deep in places, making it near impossible to walk, or keep a chain saw sharp.

After about a month or so, we're almost done with this job site, and most of our work is moving from log deck, to log deck loading out all the remnants, more or less cleaning up. To expedite things, we decided that instead of securing the loader every time we moved it, we would just pull up the out riggers. Lonnie would remain up in the roost while I drove the Mack truck it was mounted on to the next log deck.

We did this for a few days, and it was working out real good. Soon I'm beginning to think I'm a real good truck driver. Why, I could even back up by looking in the mirrors; this logging wasn't so bad after all. That old Mack was a pretty good rig except for it needed a jump when it was cold, and every now and again she would pop out of gear while we were backing up. I would hit the air brakes, get her stopped, double clutch the hell out of 'er, grind 'er back into reverse and carry on with our task. Except for the time that the air cannister blew up!

We were just about done with the job, so naturally that was cause for celebration at the tavern after work. The Mack had just popped out of gear again, and as I applied the air brakes I heard a whooshing sound. A little flag dropped down in the windshield with writing on it, it said, "WARNING: low air pressure". Low air pressure my ass, we had no air pressure!

Well ain't this nice, "here we go" I thinks to myself, the old Mack is out of gear rolling backwards, with no brakes. Meanwhile Lonnie old buddy is up in the cab wondering why I'm going so fast! All of this happened in a matter of seconds, we were sure enough in a pickle and getting in deeper all the time.

The road had about a 5 or 6% grade to it, a straight shot for 1/4 mile, then a 90 degree turn at the bottom where it levels out. There in the road sits the log truck with about a third of a load on his bunks, oblivious to our predicament.

An old friend of mine, Jack Ross of Brookings, OR. once summed it up as well as anyone. He quipped that the worst fate that could befall an aviator, was to run out of altitude and ideas at the same time, now I know how he felt.

This was really turning out to be shitty day, I was doing about 25 mph in reverse, excuse me, neutral, and going faster and faster! I wasn't really a truck driver, but I had enough sense to know that there is no way this rig is going to make that corner, top heavy and with a log truck in the middle of the road. Numb nuts Lonnie would be killed for sure, and it wouldn't do me much good either.

I remember scaring the hell out of the cutters as they were walking down the road to their rigs. They were all yelling for me to slow down! "I wish to Christ I could slow down, assholes," I hollered back as they dove for safety. By now Lonnie had surmised that something was amiss and had started lowering the outriggers to try and stop us, I never knew this until it was all over.

Well, I'd had about enough of this shit, and decided that my best bet was to try and ease 'er into the ditch and bank to get her stopped, so I did.

When those out riggers hit that rock wall, all hell broke loose. Rocks flew like shrapnel, severing hydraulic lines and radiator hoses. The radiator itself was blown to bits. Rocks had pierced the oil pan of the loader engine, fortunately there was no fire, but one hell of a lot of smoke and steam. The front wheels of the truck got ripped right out from underneath of her, the old gal was a hurtin' for certain.

I seemed to be intact, so I bailed out to check on Lonnie. He was mad as hell and nuttier than squirrel shit, then everyone shows up all at once. The cutters, log truck driver, and the rest of our crew, and everyone of the son of a bitches is hollering and yelling at me!

After the assholes shut up for a little bit, I explained to them what had happened. They checked the wreck out and found I was telling the truth. The brakes had dynamited, but they were so worn and out of adjustment it did little or no good.

Lonnie and I were summoned to go on the carpet before the owner of the mill. We pleaded our case as best we could. I was credited with making the best of a bad situation, and probably saving Lonnie's life, but we were also reprimanded for moving the truck around with the operator in the cab.

We were down for two months while they put the old girl back together ... shit happens.

HOOKTENDER'S HEAVEN

I was worn out from diggin' choker holes out on the riggin,
When a widow maker fell, and conked me on my head.
I began to cuss and yell, then I staggered 'round and fell,
And when I came to, I noticed I was dead.

Judgement day was finally here, I was prayin' hard for beer,
And hoping for a pardon for my wrongs.
There was music in the air, and Angels everywhere,
Strummin' on harps, and singin' purdy songs.

Then I began to thinkin', 'bout my heathen ways and drinkin',
And ponderin' what lay ahead for me.
When St. Peter up 'n said, "son, seein's how you're dead,
I know the place where you gotta be".

With that the trumpets blared, my eyes got big and stared,
At old growth, fell and bucked, laying all in lead.
All the choker holes was dug, I had a pearl handled bug,
I was so tickled I damn near pee'd.

Then my jaw went slack, there was Haulback Jack,
Old Growth Gus and Whistle Punk Pete;
There was Marlin Spike Mike, old One Eyed Ike,
Rowdiest bunch you're ever gonna meet.

Buzz Martin was a singin', while the rigging he was slingin',
Slacked new chokers down to Mackinaw McGabe.
But my biggest thrill of all, was meetin' up with old Paul,
And his trusty side kick, the blue ox Babe.

No jaggers there for us to hold, the choker bells was solid gold,
The weather always bright and clear.
The camp was like a dude resort, the fancy, high falutin' sort,
And the cricks was all full of beer.

Well, this weren't so awful bad, tougher times I've surely had,
Don't have to fret no more 'bout dyin'.
Fact is, this side is mighty swell, tight logs and hang ups down in hell,
Now I've grown wings and took up flyin'.

PARDS

When times get rough and you've had enough,
And the goin' gets real hard.
It's times like these a man really needs,
Someone to call his pard.

He's a kindred spirit, few things come near it,
A true friend, right to the end.
There's spats and fall outs along the way,
But always a fence there to mend.

Who do you call when you're down and out,
When there ain't no beans in the pot?
And who else would stand back to back,
And give it all they've got?

All the troubles on your mind, no matter the kind,
A pard is there for you.
Tested by time, a treasure to find,
A pard is both tried and true.

I've said it once, and I'll say it again,
Life is an uphill climb.
And if you're lucky enough, to find a pard,
Try and keep him for all of time.

TRAPPINGS

Trappings tell the story, of that which comes to pass,
Of battles fought and wars that can't be won.
Lifetimes spent pursuing fortunes to amass,
Wondering if you'll get the chance to have a little fun.

Trappings are your pride and joy, your worth, some people claim,
They tell the world what you're all about.
Trappings are your resume, your reference and good name,
Trappings tell the truth, beyond a shadow of a doubt.

Trappings are the clothes you wear, the jewelry you adorn,
The paintings hanging on your parlor walls.
Trappings are your legacy, though some you hate and scorn,
They focus on the climb, ignoring all the falls.

Trappings tell what you are, or what you wish you were,
Or what you think that might have been.
Trappings sometimes don't amount, to what you would prefer,
And pitfalls lay in wait of unsuspecting men.

Trappings are for old men, grown men, and for boys,
There's Trappings for each and everyone.
A man's character is judged by the measure of his toys,
But Trappings all are worthless, when the race is finally run.

CAMP FIRE JOURNEYS

There are tales untold, yet somehow one remembers,
They echo 'round in your head for quite a long time.
I watched the world unfold in my campfire's embers,
If you'll pardon my intrusion, I'll share my little rhyme.

I lazed one night, by the campfire bright,
Staring down coals that glowed cherry red.
When the whole wide world suddenly unfurled,
Within the narrow confines of my head.
I bore witness to the mystery, of time, space, and history,
I saw it all, right there in the fire.
There was greed and lust, honor and trust,
There was hope and despair, amid wanton desire.

I saw drought and the flood, the battles and the blood,
The gift of life, and the mercy in death.
I saw paupers and kings, angels with wings,
Men unworthy of their next breath.
All creation was my range, what if anything would I change,
And should I, if I could?
Seemed the further I traveled, the more I unraveled,
Often I wondered, if this was good.

I saw men toil, for the gold and oil,
They went half mad, when their money was gone.
They lay broken and shattered, unaware of what mattered,
Void of spirit, withered and wan.
I sailed the high seas, I caught the disease,
Of men born under a wondering star.
One truth rang sure, no matter where they were,
They couldn't help being who they are.

In the fire there were faces, smiles and embraces,
Vermin in the shadows, up to no good.
There were heads hung in shame, deeds to rank to claim,
Decent folks getting by, anyway they could.

It wasn't hard to tell that all roads led to hell,
Everybody there had got to make their choice.
Their days had nearly passed, when they finally saw at last,
They should have listened to that little voice.

It seemed the longer I stared, the less I cared,
For the world I gazed upon.
Blindly I groped, I prayed and I hoped,
That I'd travel forever, and the fire blazed on.
I saw monsters and a ghost, I was luckier than most,
I stirred the fire, and sparks filled the skies.
I heard the angels sing, the church bells ring,
I heard the mongrel races and the truths in their lies.

I saw all of God's creatures, stark and void of features,
Dancing in the flames and writhing in the coals.
They all looked up at me, as if they couldn't see,
That it was too late for me to save their souls.
In the fire, time and space ran amok a fitful pace,
Hell bent to get there, but not a clue to where.
On the fire burned, my heart, it ached and yearned,
My stone cold face, turned red from the glare.

I was blessed and kissed, by the rain and mist,
I lay my bed on the billowing clouds.
I've spent my days in a wilderness haze,
Far, far away from the maddening crowds.
And I felt a bit unnerved, why had I deserved,
To see in the fire, the way that things are.
And I can go anywhere, unbridled, free of care,
And I rule o'er the world, from my throne atop a star.

COUGAR

Predator silent, sleek and swift,
Like smoke, through the woods you drift.
Eyes that glitter, glow, and shine,
Stealthy stalking, 'neath the pine.
Deadly games, you play each day,
As intended, nature's way.
O'er rocky ledge, cliff, and dale,
Nocturnal prowler, shrill you wail.
Feline recluse, domain secluded,
Human wrath so long eluded.
No fear you know, save for man,
Long reign supreme, in God's plan.

CHANGES

Once we were many, standing tall and proud,
A little rambunctious and usually too loud.
Perched upon a spring board with a misery whip,
Good ole boys that didn't take much lip.

They used beasts of burden to skid their logs,
Worked 'em all day, and worked 'em like dogs.
They cussed 'em, prod 'em, they lashed at their flanks,
Why, they had their own kids a greasin' the planks.

Steam donkeys and spar trees, became steel towers,
Chainsaws did in minutes, what took cross cuts hours.
By and by, we'd gotten pretty damn good,
They were standing in line to buy our wood.

Then in the 80's they found the spotted owl,
That was it, you should have heard 'em howl.
By the 1990's, they had all but shut us down,
For every hippie in a tree, there were ten on the ground.

And all these new comers with all them degrees,
Told us loggers to quit cuttin' down trees.
So I'm off to school to go sit in some class,
Gonna get real smart, then sit on my ass.

Loggers are now villains in my home town,
There ain't but a few of us left around.
When the wind blows hard, the big firs bend,
Poor old loggers got no coins to spend.

THE BULL WHACKER BLUES

Get off'n your ass, and up on your feet,
You sorry bag 'o bones, you tired ol' beast.
Step lively, or I'll turn you into camp meat,
Or worse yet, leave you for the buzzard's feast.

I know that your old, but we've logs to yard,
You're limpin' a bit, must be them old hips.
They're greasin' the planks, hup-ho my old pard,
I'm hearing the twang of those misery whips.

Slip with your partner, now into the yoke,
It's time that we hit that old skid road.
Now pick up your pace, you sorry old poke,
Though I don't like it, I'll give you the goad.

The team's a waitin', they're rattlin' the chains,
The flies are a buzzin' and the dung is knee deep.
Your sores are bleeding, can't wait for the rains,
Up and at 'em old boy, go earn your keep.

We've a grade to pull boys, long, hard and steep,
Lean into it, heave ho and give it your best.
The earth is our garden, its bounty we reap,
We've miles to go 'till we lay down and rest.

The lines are tight, and the blocks are a squeakin'
The whips are crackin', your bellows echo loud.
The team's lathered up, their bones are a creakin'
The whacker and his team, steadfast and proud.

We've made it to the top, but our job ain't over,
Now we've got to get down the other side.
Rest a minute boys, and munch on some clover,
Take 'er nice and slow, or we'll go for a ride.

Just another day boys, our backs swayed and bent,
Off to your hovel, for a night in the hay.
We made it again, but were tired and spent,
Sweet dreams to the teams, soon comes the day.

141

THE CHILL

It comes and goes so fast they say,
This thing we call the chill.
Widow makers come down every day,
And when they hit, they kill.

The hair on your neck really does stand up,
And your palms, they really do sweat.
Your knees will shake, and you may throw up,
Your britches might even get wet.

Try as you may, you can't dodge your fate,
When things come crashing down the hill;
Sometimes you feel like it's too late,
That's when you get the chill.

The chill lurks behind every stump,
You know it's never too far away,
Leave you on the ground, in a lifeless lump,
Never will know, when it's your day.

Day after day, you put in your time,
You try not to get too relaxed;
'Cause when you do, for no reason or rhyme,
Your number comes up, and you get whacked.

The closer the call, the harder the fall,
Stone cold, all alone in your bed.
The shakes and cold sweats, come to call,
You know damn well, you should be dead.

Who can say what makes a man stay,
And look death in the face for a living.
He learns to live life day by day,
And he knows mistakes are unforgiving.

THE PULLOVER

Ah, the pull over. No doubt one of the highlights of my not so stellar career of endless elbow bending binges. Again we return to that cozy little hamlet nestled in the foothills on the west side of the Cascades: Sweet Home, Oregon.

My cohort, Lonnie and myself were in the employ of Flying Scotsman, this was a balloon logging outfit, an off chute of Bohemia Inc. Our job was high up in the Cascades on Gold Creek, a small tributary of Quartzville Creek, which is all within the Santiam water shed.

Do to its remote location, Lonnie and I elected to live on the job, in a 1950's vintage camp trailer, on the banks of Quartzville Creek we would spend the work week there and go home on the weekends.

We did however, from time to time venture into Sweet Home for a bit of barstool logging, such is how it was on that fateful night. We had been previously thrown out of most of the taverns in town and refused service at the rest. So having no place left to go we decided it was time to head 'er back up in the brush to our little home away from home, on wheels.

Having been down this road before, we had the foresight to buy some beer for the ride home, in advance of being 86'd by civilization. We removed our ice chest of now chilled to perfection beer from the trunk and placed it in the back seat for easy access. We were no sooner in the car and Lonnie, true to form, passes out in the passenger seat, and is for all intents and purposes dead to the world. I am always the designated driver, for just that reason.

We were in Lonnie's car, a 1964 Plymouth Belvedere that looked as if it was just snatched from the jaws of the crusher. It was an eyesore, to speak kindly of it. The only working headlight was permanently aimed skyward, as if we were spot lighting for geese. If it had a muffler on it, it wasn't hooked up, and the windshield was cracked so bad it looked like a big spider web.

Knowing that small town cops become easily bored and are looking for something to do, I elect to get out of Dodge without incident. After stopping at the parking lot of The Timbers Inn on the east end of town, I make sure Lonnie buddy had his door secured, we sneak out of town, and head for the hills.

As we pass The Pointe Restaurant, I am much relieved that there are no cops in the parking lot, as is the case sometimes, and continue on highway 20 to our turn off to Quartzville Creek.

As I approach the turn off, I cannot believe my eyes. There in all his glory sits one of Oregon's finest, no shit, an Oregon State Trooper, and there's not a damn thing I can do. To try and outrun him would be not only futile, but stupid and just land me in more trouble than I was already in.

My only option available was to proceed onward like I was doing nothing wrong. So I did, and guess what, it didn't work. He was on me like bark on a tree, blue lights flashing and the whole Mary Ann. I resolved to go peacefully and wheeled over and shut her down.

The trooper strolls up to the old Plymouth, giving it the once over with his Mag Lite and shaking his head all the while. I figured we were in for a long night, rolled down the window, and cheerfully greeted the officer. He acts like he didn't even hear me and keeps looking at the Plymouth, still shaking his head. He walked all the way around it, shaking his damn head the whole time. I know she wasn't much to look at, but I've seen worse, I just can't remember when.

At long last he makes his way to the driver's side, again I cheerfully greet him, and again, there is no reply. He directs his light on Lonnie old buddy who is still dead to the world, (thank God).

After that he looks to the floorboards which are carpeted in empty beer cans, then to the back seat where our well stocked cooler is, and more empty beer cans.

Finally he acknowledges my presence and I display my driver's licence for him. He goes through the whole damn routine again. Lonnie, the floor boards, the back seat. He looks at his watch, then off he goes again, walking around the Plymouth still shaking his head. I'm beginning to wonder if this guy has a nervous disorder of some sort.

Again he returns to the driver's window, where I offer my licence to him again, once more he shines his light on Lonnie, the empties, the cooler and glances at his watch.

I'm startled when I hear him finally speak, "where are you boys

144

headed," he queried. "Back up to our job site on Quartzville Creek", I sheepishly replied.

"Well, good luck to you, I'm not up to dealing with you two losers tonight", and off he went, still shaking his head. He got into his cruiser and sped off as fast as he could go, headed for town!

Needless to say I was both shaken and relieved at the same time. I reached around to the cooler, got a beer, popped a top and headed for the barn, nice and easy like. To this day Lonnie doesn't remember a thing and thinks I made it all up!

SHOW 'N' TELL

The school marm one day was heard to say,
To her classroom full of kids:
"Go home and bother, divulge from your father,
What was the kind of work that he did".

They read and recited, they got all excited,
Then up steps the son of a logger now dead.
The lad felt uneasy, kind of funny and queasy,
You could hear in his voice the pride as he read.

"Why I start each day, the same old way,
By wakin' the rooster up.
I'm two hours gone, got cork boots on,
And rarin' to go when the sun gets up.

I put in my hours, under high lead towers,
In a driving rain with no coat.
I set inch chokes, while I laugh and tell jokes,
On ground too steep for a mountain goat.

I'll turn straight in to a howlin' wind,
In the muck clean up to my knees.
I've spent hours untold in woods so cold,
If I stopped, I'd surely freeze.

I've coiled miles of wire, fought many a fire,
And notched my share of stumps.
I've seen blood spilled, seen men killed,
And had my share of bruises and lumps.

I've been baked and broiled, for hours I've toiled,
In heat not fit for a beast.
Through it all, I stood proud and tall,
I've earned my eternal peace."

HIGH HOPES

There's a young lad with his eyes agleam,
A grin that touches both his ears,
As he tries to walk, in caulk boots he can't lift;
But all the boy can do is dream,
'Cause he's a little short on years,
But every night he prays he'll have the gift.

At the crummy stop he waits each night,
For the crews that come rolling into town,
Bragging of their daring feats that day.
Those beat up crummies, such a pretty sight,
Sliding sideways, through the turn around,
If the old lady seen him now, what would she say?

The door flies open and the crew falls out,
Reeking of those old familiar smells,
Sweat, tobacco, Diesel fuel and beer.
He's having fun now, there's no doubt,
Playing with them choker bells,
Or in the crummy, trying to find a gear.

Schoolin's not his cup of tea,
He gets bored as hell indoors,
Hes not known for doing too much study.
In the woods, is where he wants to be,
Blazing hot, or when it pours,
Bruised and battered, all beat up and muddy.

His plans, dear mother strives to change,
Though hard she tries, it's all in vein,
Some things are best just left alone.
A logger's life to most is strange,
Why wallow in the mud and rain,
And worry if you're gonna make it home.

THE LOGGER'S WIFE, AKA THE OLD LADY

I've rhymed and chimed and told you about,
The woes of a logger's life.
Won't you sit a spell, for now I must tell,
The woes of the logger's wife.
She's up before him, in dawn's early dim,
Fixing up coffee, breakfast, and lunch.
It's her thankless chore, she does it and much more,
She plays it by ear, and rolls with the punch.

There's young un's to tend, and britches to mend,
A house to clean, and groceries to get.
All those stories to hear, the smell of cheap beer,
Piles of clothes, all muddy and wet.
The kids are in school, she married a fool,
No matter what she can't get ahead.
He's not home and it's late, she's gettin' irate,
She's callin' the bars, and seeing red.

Her life is a test, but she gives it her best,
Day in and out, she lives on the run.
There's a garden to grow, and lawns to mow,
The old lady's day never is done.
She does what she must, in good times or bust,
To keep her family on even keel.
Come hell or high water, he's damn glad he's got her,
A heart of pure gold and nerves like steel.

She hopes and she prays, that one of these days,
She might be able to slow down her pace.
But 'till then she'll run, and forego her fun,
No time for frills, feathers and lace.
Sometimes she wonders, amid mishaps and blunders,
What's the reward for all of her strife.
But she knew from the start, when he won her heart,
Nothing comes easy, for an old logger's wife.

PRODIGAL SONS

Prodigal sons, of your conservative fathers,
Like they, were you washed in the blood?
Your mind's a clutter of trivial bothers,
You run from hard work, and are scared of the mud.
Is your word any good, is your handshake firm,
Has your mettle been summoned, put to the test?
When it hits the fan, do you stand tall or squirm,
Are you bad as the worst, or as good as the best?

It's hard to make sense of your insolent babble,
Would you give of yourself, to keep others free?
Do you live life in earnest, or linger and dabble,
You've two good eyes, but still you can't see.
You measure your worth, in material things,
Your hands are smooth as a new baby's ass.
You fly through life, like a star that fate slings,
You live for tomorrow, and can't face your past.

Who am I, they say, to be Judge,
I'm a father to sons, who don't know themselves.
I'm right and you're wrong, and I will not budge,
My name isn't Santa, and you're not my elves.
You're Johnny come lately, if you show up at all,
You can't brave the storm, nor scale the peak.
You're music's so loud, you can't hear me call,
You're shiftless, aimless, and pitifully weak.

I'm calling and calling, my sons can't you hear,
My job is to show you the right road to take.
It's true that life's hard, but you've nothing to fear,
Use faith as your vessel son, swim in the wake.

DADDY'S MONEY

All the gold and riches Daddy made,
Have done to me more harm than good.
The calling of a dollar, I eagerly obeyed,
But happiness was something, I never understood.

How I loved the lime light, and company of rich folks,
The prodigal son, who played so well the part of clown.
I keep them all in stitches, plied with drink and jokes,
As I lead my jolly caravan all about the town.

Fast cars and faster women were at my beckoned call,
A snap of my fingers lay them at my feet.
Though I sat tall in the saddle, I was riding for a fall,
Never could play by the rules, always had to cheat.

Once I had a wife, she was a keeper I would wager,
Had hair of silk, and eyes that twinkled bright;
But my antics and behavior, served only to enrage her,
She left my gilded tower when she finally saw the light.

But my friends, they still love me, I've got lots of money,
When I foot the bill, they all tell me that I'm swell.
The guys all slap my back, and the girls call me honey,
Sure, I'm always smiling, truth is, I live in hell.

I've never had a callous, upon my hands so soft,
Never spent a day toiling in a filthy ditch.
I never saw the wonder in the moon and stars aloft,
Never had to work or worry, never found my niche.

This misery is killing me, somehow it all must end,
I'm headed for oblivion, down this road I trod.
I need so much, but most of all I need a friend,
He's been there all along for me, I found my friend in God.

THE ADVENTURES OF PAULINE

Looking over a career spanning twenty some years as a beer swilling logger, one can well imagine the difficulty in trying to pin down any one particular low point. However, having had such an esteemed career I do have a lot of experiences to draw from! Here's a few I can remember!

Back in the early eighties, Woodrow and me figured that our line splicing skills were a little on the rusty side and that we should get our buddy to give us a little tutoring in the fine art of line splicing and putting in eyes. Our buddy, whom we'll call Paul, reluctantly agreed to our request, and a time was scheduled.

Now Woodrow and myself, being the gentlemen that we were, figured it was only polite that we should bring along a little liquid refreshment in case we got thirsty in splicing class!

Well, it turns out that Paul wasn't real happy about it, so we naturally set out to change his dismal out look on things. It took us awhile, but after a few trips down to the corner market for more beer we had our mentor every bit as lubed up as we were, if not a little more. Splicing class was going real good, we had a splice for all occasions, with two left over!

We had pyramids of beer cans built on Mrs. Paul's nice dinner table. There were cans strewn from hell to breakfast and a cloud of smoke hung in the room that would rival any dive that comes to mind!

Woodrow and I were a real hit with the kids! They loved the hell out of us. We had them hootin' 'n' hollerin' and cussin' right along with the crew!

A good time was being had by all and we reveled in it and savored of the moment, the comaraderie, the "espirit de corps", but then the door opens and in steps Mrs. Paul.

Mrs. Paul is all decked out in this fancy business woman suit, and is some kind of high falutin' legal begal of sorts and she's not real happy about our splicing class in her house! This poor woman can't believe what she's seeing. Then Woodrow sticks out his hand, introduces himself as "Snag" and falls down in a heap right at her feet!

This of course is very amusing to me, as evidenced by my leg slapping and subsequent seizures. Now would be a good time to interject a heretofore undisclosed fact about our host and splicing teacher Paul, and that is that he had a slight speech impediment.... He stuttered a bit, not real bad, but tonight in light of all the excitement Paul's stuttering was a little more pronounced. Actually, you could say it was a lot more unpronounced.

The poor bastard couldn't even talk! He just sat there going Ga.... Ga.... Ga.... Ga, I think he was trying to say her name, no matter though. She'd had her fill of us, and left with a bee in her bonnet and her bloomers in a bunch!

We found out later why she was so pissed off, it was because her kids that liked us so much were in drug rehab!!! Shit we didn't know; damn pecker head Paul should of told us.

Old Paul was a fairly good timber cutter. From time to time Woodrow and I would be out of work for one reason or another and we'd work for Paul cutting for a day or two. We loved it and Paul seemed to like our company because he sure put up with a lot of shit from us!

Now old Paul liked to smoke and chew, he did 'em both at the same time. If he ever quit it would probably kill the guy.

There we'd be in August, 1:00 closure in effect, out in the middle of the unit, and there's Paul standing there with a camel in his mouth showing Woodrow and I our strip to cut. Telling us how he wanted it done, and taking about fifteen minutes to do it. We were loving the hell out of this, as we were getting paid by the hour.

So, as soon as Paul flicks his cigarette in the brush Woodrow would remind him of the fire danger and point out all these puffs of smoke from Pauls chain smoking. We'd go and put out all of Paul's little fires and then Woodrow or I would inevitably ask Paul if he would go over the plan of action one more time with us!

Of course, he would be happy to and whole cycle would be gone through again and again!

We got so we could spend an hour or more a day, just smoking Paul's cigs, and going over the plan!

I remember one day, a year or so before our splicing school adventure, Old Paul and I were working for the same outfit. He was cutting and I was the landing man. Each morning he would pass through my landing on the way to his strip. We would trade insults and disparaging comments about each others wife and mother and each go on about his day.

This particular morning, Paul has an air of confidence about him. Something was different.... why, he has on a brand new outfit.... the whole Mary Ann, brand spankin' new. If that ain't enough to get the neighbors talking, he's got a brand new Husky to boot.... a nice big one.

What's the occasion I inquire? No reply, he just smiled and whistled, on his way to work.

A few hours later we heard a pretty big tree go down off in Paul's direction, which isn't unusual.

But out of the dust, we see this figure kind of staggering sideways and just generally not real steady on his feet.

Closer observation reveals the figure to be Paul. He is just beat to dog shit, shirt and pants shredded right on his body, suspenders ripped right off, there was chunks out of his corks.

He had cradled in his arms the remnants of his new saw, it was just horrible, a complete loss.

Poor Paul was nuttier than squirrel shit, he just kept mumbling over and over "she set back on me fellers, she set back on me".

Poor son of a bitch, he was cut up and bruised. He looked like he'd been shit off a cliff by a rabid dog. We sat him down, got him together and came to find out he had a big fir snag go over and slab on him.

To this day he can't tell you what the hell happened or where he went wrong! The poor bastard was goofy the rest of the day. It wasn't long after that someone found the sacred and endangered spotted owl, boy, were we ever in for a surprise.

HARD DAY AT THE OFFICE

Have you stood outside the circle boys,
Watched guylines dance, seen the tower quiver?
Have you heard the lines, make that noise,
Pulled haywire through a coffee colored river?

Have you blown your choker holes with powder,
Numbed your hands on frozen bells of steel?
Can you spot wild riggin', not let 'em crowd 'er,
Worked all day and never took a meal?

Have you heard a tired old yarder groan,
Had a widow maker land right at your feet?
Have you worked all day chilled to the bone,
Do you still think a crummy smells oh so sweet?

Have you dodged the choker bells a flyin',
Had the haulback siwash past your head?
Have you seen a new made widow cryin',
Walked away, knowing you should be dead?

Have you been in the bight, when a tight line parts,
Been on the saw when a big fir barber chairs?
Have you grabbed a line adorned with darts,
Or fallen down a rocky flight of stairs?

Have you been hung up, hog jawed for sure,
Mucked around the guylines in the rain?
Been thumped so hard, you forgot who you were,
But finished out the day, in spite of all the pain?

A hard day at the office friend, city life got you down?
Come and romp with me, out among the trees.
We'll wonder o'er the hillsides, forget that ugly town,
Dig our choker holes, down on bended knees.

There won't be no lattes, cappuccinos, or croissants,
Just lots of mud, and then more mud.
The boss said he wants more logs and he gets what he wants,
While we foot the bill, with our sweat and blood.

PEACE

Peace you'll find, is a state of mind,
You see, it's mainly in your head.
That's what everyone is trying to find,
But they run out of time instead.

The smell and feel of wood heat,
On a cold and dreary morn.
Wood split up and all stacked neat,
There's peace in the work that keeps you warm.

Peace is in that tired feeling,
You've grown to love each night.
Peace in playing the hand life is dealing,
And knowing you've played it right.

Peace lives in each and everyone,
Pity them that never find it.
Wars not waged are never won,
No spoils reward the violent.

There's even peace in the sound of thunder,
And the lightning can strike your soul.
The crash and flash are works of wonder,
Hear it echo, rumble and roll.

There's the peace a tended garden lends,
To live off your own lands.
There's peace in the pain of a back that bends,
And love in the touch calloused hands.

156

LEAVING HOME

Over time this place has grown on me,
It's taken right a hold,
It's firmly rooted, deep down in my soul.
This is where I need to be,
As I turn gray and old,
'Neath the sturdy oak atop the knoll.

These ruts I wore, the paths I trod,
My mark is everywhere,
Every shrub and tree I know by heart.
I've endured by the grace of God,
Through thick and thin, joy and despair,
But all too soon, this place and I must part.

The weathered barn and wood shack,
The swing down by the pond,
All have been my haunts down through the years,
The beauty in the woods out back,
And all that lies beyond,
Just the thought of leaving here, brings me close to tears.

The sagging gates and windmills,
Old trucks that up and died,
Tools and men alike, all turn to dust.
Let the chips fall where they will,
By nature's law, all things abide,
Sometimes she seems a little bit unjust.

And now the sun is riding low,
And dimmer grows the sky,
It's true that all good things must end.
These simple truths I've come to know,
As my time to leave draws nigh,
This place has always been my closest friend.

The grim reaper plies his timeless trade,
The minstrel sings at our request,
Here I will remain, until my final breath.
And when our bed at last gets made,
And comes the time for us to rest,
We'll live forever after the formality of death.

157

BART

I was tinkering in the front yard one day,
More or less just scratchin' my butt.
When moseyin' down the old highway,
Came a half starved, pitiful mutt.

I must have been in a pretty good mood,
Because I gave the poor guy a snack.
He growled and snapped and wolfed it down,
Then took off, without lookin' back.

No one can say to this very day,
What made the ol' boy pick me.
He must have been used to having his way,
So companions we would be.

Fate had given us to each other,
No fee was there to pay.
Time would bond us just as brothers,
We lived our lives day by day.

He'd wander off for days on end,
But he always made his way back.
No harm my way, dare any man send,
For fear of his attack.

The jingle of keys, he could hear for a mile,
It would bring him hell bent on the run.
Into the back of the Ford he'd pile,
For ol' Bart, nothing else was as fun.

He's pissed on my leg, crapped in the truck,
Swiped a steak or two off the grill.
He's been shot at and hit, just missed by luck,
I thought it was cats, that was so hard to kill.

He could tell the sound of the neighbor's truck,
From far off down the way.
That really got ol' Bart riled up,
He tried to kill him every day.

I'd been out a little late one night,
Bar stool loggin' with the guys.
When I got home, no Bart was in sight,
And the tears welled up in my eyes.

I'd taken a corner a little fast I 'spose,
Pitched ole Bart right out of the truck.
All it did was skin up his nose,
Ol' Bart never ran out of good luck.

I'd stopped one night at the topless bar,
For just one beer and no more.
When I heard a dog was chasing cars,
And wouldn't let people in the door.

Ol' Bart stayed on for twelve good years,
Never once did he let me down.
Then one day we faced our fears,
Put our friend, ol' Bart in the ground.

Sometimes I swear he's in the back of the Ford,
That was his favorite place to be;
Every now and again, I still thank the Lord,
For the time that he gave ol' Bart-n-me.

TIME

I wonder if someone would please be so kind,
As to explain to me all about time.
It comes and it goes, it came and it went,
Who's to say how time is well spent.

Should you spend it in the haze downtown at the bars,
Or laying in the grass trying to count the stars?
Some spend their's seeking fortune and fame,
Others could care less, to them, life's a game.

Should there be a price for all the time one needs,
And how is your life measured, in time or by deeds?
So time is money, now ain't that funny, no one ever told me.
I've no spare time, and I can't spare a dime, I'm still as broke as can be.

Not to run out of time, until your time's up, that's the name of the game,
When your time is all gone, life goes on, time is always the same.
Maybe in time I'll have some time ,to slow down a little and breathe,
But by that time it'll be too late, and time for me to leave.

CUTTIN' FIREWOOD

Many were the times when I put beans in the kettle by cutting fire-wood when we were laid off from logging for one reason or another. We would always yard up sound snags and buckskins in the unit for just that purpose, knowing that the logging business is chicken one day and feathers the next. One could say that was our backwoods unemployment insurance policy.

I always preferred do go it alone for a number of reasons, the main one being I didn't have to split the take with anyone. Another reason was a lot of guys would like to get drunk while doing it and I was always dead set against working and drinking at the same time. It's just too damn dangerous. Don't misunderstand me, I've guzzled enough beer in my day to float a battleship and pissed enough to drown the crew, but I did one or the other, very seldom did I mix the two.

I liked to take my boys with me when they got old enough to work. I liked the free labor, but it didn't take long before they figured out there was always something a little better to do than cut firewood with the old man. So that left just me and old Bart, my dog. Bart was the best dog a man ever had, dumber than shit, but he was my true pard. Our esca-pades together, spanning twelve years I will never forget.

One time I was cutting on an old landing east of Oakridge, OR. I had finished up loading the last of the wood and I laid on the horn to call Bart in, as it was time to head 'er home. He didn't care for all the noise of the chain saw, so he would take off out in the woods and amuse himself chasing critters and what not. On occasion he would run into a porcu-pine or a hornet's nest and he would come in a bit early, on the run with his tail between his legs!

This particular day was uneventful, with exception of meeting an-other woodcutter on our way out of the draw that our wood lot was nestled in. That in itself is not unusual, but by coincidence we each had white '66 Ford pick up trucks. We stopped briefly in the logging road

162

and chatted a bit then went about our business. They continued downward to the landing to cut their load and I went upward towards town. Then I remembered that I hadn't put the required Forest Service tags on my load, so I continued on a bit to a flat spot and got out to tag the wood.

As I got out of my truck, I heard a horn blaring and voices hollering and yelling and carrying on like there was some kind of disaster unfolding... there was!!

Now you remember earlier I remarked that old Bart wasn't real sharp, you're about to see how I came to that conclusion. Unbeknownst to me, Bart had saw this other truck and being damn near identical to mine, the old bastard had apparently thought it was mine and jumped from my truck into theirs! It should be noted that Bart was a fiercely loyal dog, a Black Forest German Shepard with tan socks on all fours. He was very large and intimidating when he thought that someone or something was threatening me or "his" truck. Simply put, he would tear the living hell out of anyone doing anything he took as a threat.

So, there was old Bart down there guarding "his" truck. Those poor wood cutters were hollering for all they were worth, trying to get my attention! I waved at them, acknowledging their predicament and headed their way, on the double. The look on old Bart's face was priceless when I pulled up, I honestly to this very day, believe he was embarrassed, and rightly so.

He cocked his head, looked at me and then looked at my Ford, looked at the other woodcutters and then jumped out of their truck and came over to me with his tail between his legs, as if to apologize. I loaded him up in the back of the Ford and put his chain on him and off we went to go sell our wood.

Another one of Bart's little escapades occurred during the delivery of a load of wood. In an effort to keep our expenses down, and realize a little more profit from our efforts, most of the local boys would park on the corner of 18th and Chambers Streets in Eugene, and offer our wood to the public. First come, first served, this way we avoided having to pay for an ad in the paper.

Anyone looking for wood to buy would stop there, a deal would be made, and the woodcutter followed the buyer to where it was to be delivered. It is still like that to this day. I can recall going home without selling only a couple of times in over 20 years.

This particular day I had sold a load to a pretty, affluent, older gal. Judging from our first meeting, I suspected she was a bit on the uppity side, so I was resolved to be on the best behavior becoming of an esteemed wood cutter. I could tell right off the bat she wasn't real fond of Bart, as she told me she had some cats around and to keep him in the cab.

When we arrived at her mansion, there were cats everywhere, I'll bet there were a dozen or more, this really got Bart's attention. I backed the truck to where she directed me, to off load the wood, and quickly got out of the truck making sure Bart didn't sneak out, like I know he was planning to.

The old bag paid me and left me to my task. My back was hurting a little, so I wasn't in any big hurry. I just puttered along, and by the by I finished up, secured all the tools, and went to get in the truck. Upon opening the door I am greeted by the most sickening smell you could imagine.

There in the driver's seat, is the biggest pile of dog shit in the lower forty-eight.

I am, at this point, not a very happy camper. Trying not to lose my temper, in light of where I was: I decided to just remove the seat cover, and throw it in the back of the truck, and deal with it later; but I was still pissed, and Bart knew it, he was cowering, big time.

As I was pulling on the seat cover trying to remove it, the string securing it suddenly snapped, turning it loose all at once. The result was that whole pile of dog shit was flung right into the dash board of my beloved Ford! Enraged by it all, and quite frankly momentarily out of control, I let loose with a string of expletives I wouldn't put in print. This of course panics Bart, who during my rage sees an opportunity to escape and seizes it.

As soon as Bart hits the pavement, all of those cats instantly bolt in all directions and the ensuing mayhem soon has the whole damn neighborhood outside enjoying the show. There are so many cats that Bart is just running in circles, tearing up this old bags lawn and shredding all of her plants and shrubs. Bart is indifferent to my commands to cease and desist, and has literally run amok.

By now the old bag is out there yelling and screaming for me to do something with Bart, then she heads for the house saying she's going to call the cops and the dog catcher. That was all I needed to hear. I opened the door to the truck, that is still covered with dog shit. Out of options, I have a seat right in the middle of it, fire up the Ford and get the hell out of there.

The noise of the truck starting snaps Bart back into reality, and as I look in the side mirror I see the old bastard coming on the run. I slowed to a stop so he could jump in and off we went, the whole neighborhood still back there laughing at us!!

Yes, life with Bart was interesting to say the least, but every now and then he came up on the short end of the stick. Like the time we were making a delivery in the foothills of south Eugene.

When I had a load of wood on the Ol' Ford, I had to be on the ball when I was on any kind of grade. The old girl's clutch wasn't the best and her brakes were worse, a guy had to plan and think ahead in order to avert a catastrophe. That's the way it was on this delivery, I knew where I was going, as I had delivered there before.

I had to make a right turn and go up a steep grade, it was necessary to take the corner a little fast and really pour the coal to the old girl in order to make it up the hill. As I came out of the corner I hit the throttle and all hell broke loose. I looked in my side mirror and there sat half my load in the middle of the road.

I slammed on the brakes and bailed out to see just what in the hell had happened. I heard a muffled whimpering sound coming from the wood pile in the middle of the road. It was poor Bart, buried alive in a cord wood grave!

The last two ricks (rows) of wood had tipped over backwards, hit Bart, then busted the tailgate open and the whole works wound up in the road. Quickly, I came to the aid of my fallen comrade and extricated him from his despair. Old Bart was beside himself, he was scared shitless, literally. He'd crapped all over everything, he had a cut on his ear, his front leg was buggered up a bit, but thankfully not seriously injured.

I threw the wood back on the truck, but Bart would have nothing doing getting in the back of that truck again with his little mishap still fresh on his mind. So I put him in the cab with me and there I am once again, enjoying the sweet fragrance of dog shit!

166

THE WOODCUTTER

He greets the dawn each morning,
With his heart plum full of joy,
A worn out back, and calluses of hand.
He toils at his own bidding,
With the spirit of a boy,
By his pluck, he wrests his bounty from the land.

His old truck smokes and rattles,
As he heads 'er into town,
They hear him coming, far off down the road.
His hickory shirt's in tatters,
His face is etched and brown,
Every day but Sunday, he's sure to cut a load.

Some folks, they feel pity,
While others leer disdain,
They envision him asleep down in a ditch.
He could never live in the city,
It would drive him near insane,
He sees himself well off, and filthy rich.

His old chainsaw is worn of tooth,
His axe handle, split and loose,
The tires on his old truck need replaced.
And though he wants for grace and couth,
His hairy mug is full of snoose,
It's the simple truths in life that he's embraced.

The city slickers scoff at him,
A simple waif they claim,
Undeserving of the privilege of their class.
Uncaring he ignores all them,
They're helpless and they're lame,
They wouldn't make a pimple on his ass.

And when his day is done at last,
And he's tired as hell and spent,
He mounts his easy chair and lights his pipe.
And though his life is nearly past,
His thoughts are pure heaven sent,
You'll seldom hear him whine, moan or gripe.

167

THE HIGH CLIMBER

Hi ho, hi ho, to the top he'll go,
With his tools of trade in tow.
He knows not fear as the tree top bends,
On a worn, frayed rope, his life depends.
Top 'em tall, true, and straight,
Tests his strength, and tempts his fate.
Hang the blocks and riggin' high,
Has no wife at home to cry,
Should he slip up, fall, and die.

Toppers, riggers, ply your trade,
In time your legacy will fade.
Cobwebs of steel, your trees entwined,
Through tons of blocks your cables wind.
Give those riggin' rats some lift,
They will thank you for your gift.
Set you're riggin true and fast,
Don't let this rig up be your last,
You'll all too soon, become the past.

FOREST FIRE

The sky grows dark, hear thunder heads roll,
Lightning bolts dance a jig in the sky.
The fires flare up, and soon take their toll,
The smoke roils high and the embers fly.

It's Hell on earth, it's the summer time blues,
It's out of control, it'll burn into Fall.
The grounds so hot, It'll melt your shoes,
It's a God awful sight, but its nature's call.

There's an inferno run amok, it's out of our hands,
Has mankind set the stage for his own demise?
Mother Nature will always tend to her lands,
The smoke's thick as fog, and it burns the eyes.

There's a big orange ball in the sky to the east,
It glows through the haze, like a dragon's eye.
The gibbous moon is like a pumpkin at a feast,
As it crawls like a snail, 'cross a blood red sky.

And on comes the Army, the mechanized brigade,
To quench the fires thirst and douse the wicked flames.
Hear the drone of the plane, the chopping copter blade,
God sent the lightning, but man shares the blame.

Fire is no stranger and it's not really mean,
It's been around since the dawn of the ages.
It's fires that help keep the wilderness green,
The more man meddles, the more the fire rages.

It's Hell on earth, yet from it life arises,
Fires cleanse the forests of the dying and the dead.
Now that man is here, there's bound to be surprises,
And the smoke paints the sky an eerie colored red.

BOLTCUTTER BLUES

I spent a summer on the Oregon coast ,
Cutting cedar bolts by the cord.
"I'll make a fortune", was my boast,
So off I went in my old red Ford.

Felled long ago and left to rot,
Back then they had no worth.
They lay on hillsides slick as snot,
Six feet or more in girth.

Nothing smells like cedar does,
With a little gas and sweat;
Hollow logs full of bees that buzz,
Makes the wood a little hard to get.

Chopper blades hurt your ears,
The adrenalin fills your veins.
Fly the hook out, lose your fears,
Hold on tight to steel reins.

Chainsaws, gas cans, axe and wedges,
Go everywhere with you.
Over windfalls and rocky ledges,
So much work in a day to do.

Your home's a tent, your bed's a bag,
A Coleman is your range.
Game trail highways zig and zag,
Noises in the night sound so strange.

If the week goes good like we know it should,
It's off to town we'll go;
Barstool loggin' 'till we're feeling good,
Slapped in the face, and get told, "no".

What fun we had, what a time it was,
This way of life gone past.
In looking back, I'm sad because
I knew that it could never last.

COMPANY TOWN

The old ramshackle cabins down on the flat are still there,
God only knows how, or when they might fall.
And when they do go down, likely no one will care,
They'll probably be replaced by a shopping mall.
Another way of life has come and then it's gone,
Like a handful of sawdust, tossed into the winds.
Through the portals of time, and places far beyond,
The old ways get forgotten, as a brand new age begins.

There's boards nailed up on all the windows and doors,
The rusty old stove pipes have all but fallen down.
There's bats up in the rafters, and rats run o'er the floors,
There's not much left of the old timber town.
Some cabins and the cook house burned one night,
Back into the ground from whence they came.
After all of this time, it just don't seem right,
The old company town, won't ever be the same.

I think, over there, is where the tavern used to stand,
Old Granddad told me, 'bout those Saturday nights.
They'd chortle and dance, to a washboard band,
Knock each other goofy in their barroom fights.
There's alders and briars in the railroad tracks,
The redwood water tank has fallen to the ground.
The school bell is rusted, and full of big cracks,
Souvenirs from the past, lie waiting to be found.

The porches and stairs, have mostly rotted away,
But a few old out houses still remain.
The old company store, alas, has had its day,
Standing all alone, in the cold Oregon rain.
There's the donkey and loco, sitting side by side,
Nevermore to chug and the whistle won't toot.
No one remembers when they took their last ride.
They've sat so long, they've likely taken root.

But time marches on, and change will always come,
Nothing lasts forever, all things give way to time.
But change is never easy, it's hard as hell for some,
Gold will lose its luster, and the bells will cease to chime.
But the company town is history, it's a treasure, what a find,
And though its days are numbered, it's forever in my mind.

HAND LINING

If you haven't done any hand lining yet, you haven't lived yet. Hand lining is about the crudest method of mechanized logging there is. Hand line logging incorporates what is known as "The Human Haulback". What this means, is that the yarding line is pulled right off the drum by the poor chump who is on the ground setting the chokers.

My first experience with hand lining is indelibly etched in my mind so firmly that it will never fade with time. It was out of Oakridge, Oregon, up above Hills Creek Reservoir on Packard Creek. This was Pope and Talbot land, being logged by my employer, a small gypo outfit. I forget the month, but it was winter time and there was snow ass deep to a tall logger. It was colder than a well digger's ass in the Klondike!

It was so cold first thing in the mornings that we had to fire up a propane torch to thin out the oil in the crankcase, plus, put the jumper cables on the little SJ5 we were using. I can remember laying underneath the old girl with the torch on the crankcase, then on my toes and back and forth like that, until she would start. It was a self propelled rig mounted on rubber and it was pretty mobile; (too damn mobile to suit me sometimes) It had out riggers on each corner, so that when we came to the desired spot to ply our trade we could level it up by means of the out riggers and go to logging.

The old bastard had some kind of hitch to it though. When we were on a steep grade sometimes as the lower end was raising up to level, the out rigger would just all of the sudden buckle, and down she would come with a hell of a jolt. Poor old Mert got the shit shook out of him all the time, it really used to piss the old boy off! I had to be careful about laughing at him though, because he was the owner, and he didn't think it was too funny!

Our specialty was poles and piling, some of them up to 120' long. Needless to say, these babies were worth some money and hard to come by, which meant the old man got madder than hell when one got broke.

When the weather is that cold, it was around 12 degrees for quite a spell, they break a lot easier, everything breaks a lot easier.

Here's the way hand lining worked, we would drive the Skagit along the road to where the poles were felled, after finding the desired vantage point we leveled the machine. Mert would slack the haulback drum we would attach a choker to the eye by means of a shackle and off we went, out in the brush, in all of that pretty snow! If the snow was too deep, we would go as far back as we could, hook a chunk and then drag it over the area where the wood lay covered by snow. This would knock the snow off so we could see what the hell we were after, and where they were they bucked. That being accomplished, we set about the pleasant task of setting the choker, this could be a relatively easy task, or harder than hell. If there was a space between the ground and the bottom of the log, (choker hole) it was a cinch, hook 'er up and blow three short toots on the talkie tooter and pray she isn't frozen in its bed.

If it's frozen to the ground, there are a number of tricks one can incorporate too free it up. If there is no choker hole you have to make one, this is not fun when the ground is frozen solid and your feet are too! Once the pole is hooked up and moving, the rigging man must follow it to the landing, being very careful not get hit by the log or any debris that the log upsets during its yarding. The log is followed all the way to the landing, then it is unhooked and the process is repeated until you collapse from exhaustion, or quitting time, which ever comes first!

Old Mert had quite a sense of humor in those days. He would be up in the cab of the Skagit all warm and dry. He'd see me out there shaking and shivering like a hound shittin' razor blades and ask me if I wanted to go home. "Hell, yes!" I replied "okay" he said, "we'll go home at quitting time!" Then he laughed like hell and shut his door and motioned me back out to the brush!

The log trucks that carry these 120 footers are usually provided by the company who is buying the poles, and they are, as you might imagine not an ordinary log truck. It is especially built for the task and has a computer gadget that actually steers the trailer wheels so the truck can bring them down those winding logging roads. They can only take about 6 or so poles at a time, due to weight restrictions.

On occasion, there would be enough wood in a setting that we could actually make a layout and use a haulback, like the real loggers do, That had its drawbacks also, as the roads were very short and we would work our asses off changing lines and tagging out all the time.

Most of the time, there two of us on the ground and we would take turns pulling the line out to the next pole. The other man would go out as far as necessary and help pull line, once the lead man would reach his log he would blow one short toot on his bug; this meant to stop.

The man helping to pull line then headed back up to the Skagit and took cover. If you're wondering why we would seek out cover, imagine old Mert winding on the Ol' girl, snorting a 120 footer out of the hole and encountering a hang up. The line we used was the haulback and was only 9/16" in diameter. This means that now and again it would break, and when it did it was like a mighty steel bullwhip wielded by Paul Bunyan himself. It has a report akin to a rifle shot, and if it ever hit you, you're dead in an instant.

The man on the landing learns real fast to pay attention. Mert had a steel cab protector to shield himself, but when the line broke, he liked it about as much as he did the outriggers collapsing! Once again, I had to be careful not to get caught laughing! Happy hand lining to you.

MELANCHOLY CHRISTMAS EVE

Tonight I sit contented, warmed by a crackling fire,
A wallow in the moon and stars above.
My heart is full of goodness, free of want and ire,
But all around there's turmoil, from a world in need of love.

I feel alone in this wilderness,
But shed no tears for me.
I crave this awesome emptiness,
Keeps me wild and free.

The boundless realm of earth and sky,
The vastitude of woods and plain.
The beauty in the birds that fly,
The soothing sound of falling rain.

The world has grown so small it seems,
All consumed by greed and lust.
So few of us have hopes and dreams,
Defiled and robbed of hope and trust.

Christmas, alas, is on the ropes,
Battered, pummeled, round on round;
The melting pot runs short on hopes,
Fanatics; not so tightly wound.

Virtue wanes, by leaps and bounds,
Truth obscured by lies proclaimed,
Blood runs deep in the Holy Grounds,
The innocent lay dead and maimed.

Madmen sit on thrones, pompous, wrong and regal,
All the world over, people weep and grieve.
Pagans reign supreme, and Christmas is illegal,
But none the less, I wish you all, a merry Christmas Eve.

PRAYER TO THE EAGLE

Guardian eyes from high in the skies,
Seeing all things from the top of the world.
Celestial warrior, timeless voyager,
Swift and sure as lighting bolts hurled.

All mighty Eagle, so gallant and regal,
Survivor of wars and battles untold.
Swift in flight, robust in the fight,
Eyes that sparkle and glitter like gold.

Let all evil feel your talons like steel,
Let them taste of your fury and wrath.
Rid from our life, the trouble and strife,
Lead us unto thy righteous path.

Our defender eternal, your fury infernal,
Bastion of our nation, born to be free.
Instill in us your vision, help forgo our division,
Join all of mankind in prayer and unity.

THE MUTINY

My old loggin' pard Woodrow and I had gone up to South East Alaska for logging jobs, two or three different times over the years, by and large the best holt we had was for Steve Seely.

Our camp was a large ocean going barge converted into a miniature town. It had two big Diesel power plants for electricity, berthing for the crew, kitchen and mess hall, a rec room with a vcr and tv, and the camp office, it was a pretty neat set up.

Old Woody and I had been in camp for damn near a month, without so much as a beer. We had come to the conclusion that this wasn't cuttin' 'er and we were going to do something about it, and pretty quick too!

After a short deliberation, it was decided that we would wait until after the camp superintendent had passed out, to "borrow" one of the crummies and drive the twenty miles to a remote Coast Guard station along the coast, which was purported to have a small bar to serve its contingent.

It was also rumored that the last bunch of loggers to call on them didn' leave a very good impression on them, and were asked under no uncertain terms to leave, post haste, and not return.

The only vehicle that had any keys in it was the Superintendent's pick up, so that's the one we took. After fueling it up, we were on the road to the Coast Guard station to do a little PR work and smooth out relations between the loggers and our sea faring friends, with the key to the liquor cabinet. I guess you could say we were on a diplomatic mission of sorts: Ambassadors of good will we was!

The road there was hell of a ride, one notch above a skid road, and it was a long way to the bottom. One should always be mindful that on remote logging islands in South East Alaska, there are few, in fact, there are no emergency services to be had. Undaunted, we harried our quest.

As we expected, our reception was a bit on the cool side. We did our best to play dumb, (we're naturals at it). With reservation they conceded to let us have two or three beers, make a phone call, and then be on our way; eagerly we agreed.

These swabbies had no idea who they were dealing with. Woodrow and I could bring down the roof at a nuns funeral, and we set about our task to instill some spirit in our reluctant hosts.

True to form, after we had attained our three beer limit we had them all hootin 'n' hollerin with us. Even two officers, who by means of their rank, ordered our limit of three beers be rescinded and our money would no longer be accepted. They were buying, we reveled with our new found friends in uniform.

We had this guy with us everybody called Tex, he was a very likeable guy but dumber than a doorstop, and also very gullible. He had made a phone call home which was in Medford, Oregon to talk to his wife, and a man answers the phone. We could sense that Tex is a little unnerved at first, but soon he seems his old self again and informs us that it's alright, this guy is the babysitter!

Woodrow and I exchange glances and raise our brows in a knowing manner, then dumb ass Woodrow sets out telling this poor dumb son of a bitch that it was not the baby sitter, and that his wife was playing around on him. Tex, being both drunk and stupid, soon begins to believe the idiot, and we have a bawling hillbilly on our hands who wants to kill Woodrow, and go home and do likewise to the babysitter!

I finally got Woodrow to shut his big mouth, and re-convinced Tex, that it was in fact the babysitter, and everything would be o.k. Again, being drunk and stupid, he takes the bait and says he won't kill Woodrow. In thinking back, maybe I should have let him kill the little goofball!

Along around midnight, I figured these two guys have had more than enough to drink. Then suggested we be moving along. Our hosts were in agreement, so we set about corralling Tex and Woodrow so we could be on our way. Upon hearing we were leaving, Woodrow decided he would do the driving, I tried my best to dissuade him, but to no avail, so off we went. We got in the truck and the dumb fool backed it right into a ditch about six feet deep and there we sat, screwed to a standstill. The Coast Guard crew came out and pulled us out with their front end loader. Begrudgingly, Woodrow agreed that maybe I should do the driving!

After being on the road for about five or so minutes, we discover that our purloined pick up truck has a few quirks that we weren't aware of.

When we left camp the weather wasn't that bad, a little overcast, but that is considered a dry spell in South East Alaska. As we left the Coast Guard station, the rain and fog had set in pretty good. The first thing we discover is that the windshield wipers don't work, that in itself was no big deal, I'd driven without wipers for most of my life.

What did concern me a little, was that the head lights went off. I'd had experience with that also, and as I suspected once the switch cooled down for a while they would come back on, but not for too long. I could handle that alright also, the real problem was Woodrow.

Woodrow has absolutely no patience at all, none what so ever, and that's when he's sober, after he's been drinking he is unbearable. My biggest problem at hand now was to keep his feeble minded drunken ass preoccupied, so he wouldn't want to drive again and kill us all. Normally I would have just gotten out and walked home, but that would not be advisable in bear country.

So I decided that we would roll down all the windows, open the vents, and turn the heater off in an effort to keep the switch cool. I would go like hell while the lights were on. This worked out real well until the hood flew up and damn near busted the windshield out in our faces.

It took us close to two hours to finally get back to camp, we killed the engine and coasted it right to the same spot we swiped it from, slithered like thieves in the night up to our room and passed out.

When the superintendent saw his back bumper where numbnuts had backed in the ditch, he assumed that he done it and nothing further was said of it.

HORRIBLE WAR

'Round the globe, from shore to shore,
I hear the masses loud implore;
"Death and slaughter we abhor,
Put a stop, to the horrible war".

"Let the dictator's rule remain,
To hell with slaves, and all their pain.
Leave them to their mundane chore,
Spare their death from a horrible war."

Sun bleached skeletons in the sand,
Dare not slap the murderer's hand.
Forever slam shut freedom's door,
Dare not start a horrible war.

Innocents in hordes amassed,
Beaten, tortured, shot and gassed;
Heaped in piles upon the floor,
Still, no cause for a horrible war.

Genocide of a madman's reign,
World can't hear their screams of pain.
Cannot bear the blood and gore,
Reminds them of a horrible war.

A spineless world grins and glares,
Mayhem ensues, and no one cares.
All the dead are peasants poor,
Must avoid a horrible war.

Good men cheated, loathed, and killed,
Tyrants wade, through the blood they spilled.
They shall reign for evermore,
'Cause no one wants a horrible war.

Complacent fools, protest and gloat,
Spew untruths from their filthy throat.
The true and brave will settle the score,
Cowards can't stomach a horrible war.

Shoulders strong must bear the load,
And lead the world down the road.
The long, long road to the awful chore,
The road that leads to the horrible war.

By their actions, are men gauged,
For all of time will wars be waged,
You cannot run from the horrible war,
You cannot hide from the horrible war,
Where would we be, were it not for war?
Pick your side of the horrible, horrible war.

HEALING AND DEALING

Should I heal myself, and not think of my foe,
Should a man done wrong, cast no blame?
Time heals all wounds, but who so slow,
Is to not seek the truth, to hide from the same?

We can't know what lies down the paths we trod,
Misery and despair, should be shouldered by us all.
And what of all the blood, shed in the name of God,
Why do so precious few, rise to answer the call?

We don't recall asking for all of our pain,
Would the loads that we carry, be best laid to rest?
But we, as the flowers, to grow need some rain,
To save of oneself for a more worthy test.

Where is the wisdom we should have with our years,
Should we stand our ground, or turn tail and run?
Have we lost and replaced it, with material fears,
Who then forgives us, for all that we've done?

Who makes the call, as to what's right and wrong,
Those who are monied, with their fortune and fame?
And who gives up what, so we can all get along,
Are circumstance, fate, and God's work all the same?

PIMPIN' FOR THE HOOK

When I was green, just a kid in the brush,
And hadn't yet found my nook.
The side rod said my brains was mush,
And sent me out to pimp for the hook.

He'd put a coil on his shoulders,
A block and strap in each hand.
He'd run like a deer, over logs and boulders,
Almost like he was Superman.

He'd notch a stump, or tie one back,
Change a road, or rig a tree.
There ain't too much that he can't hack,
And he don't need no help from me.

Old Hook taught me how to do some things,
That I never knew I could.
Like the pride, that sweat and hard work brings,
And the joy there is in a job done good.

With all the stuff that old Hook knows,
He oughta write a book.
When the riggin's down, and we've got woes,
We whistle for the hook.

He'll work you till you damn near drop,
You'll ache and hurt in many ways.
He'll log all day, and never stop,
There's no such thing as gravy days.

188

PRAYING FOR A BREAK DOWN

The diesel roars and the lines draw tight,
The tube is rattlin' around.
The whole damn crew is in the bight,
Prayin' like hell and huggin' the ground.

A sky car diesel powered,
With chokers hot and cold,
For some time on high lead towers,
I'd give my weight in gold.

It used to mean a road change,
Would give a man a break.
Now we just pull more line,
It's all a guy can take.

The sky cars are new fangled
With gadgetry galore.
The days of high lead gypos,
Soon will be no more.

To log this way every day,
I'd say is quite a feat.
I'm still prayin' for a break down,
And feeling damn near beat.

DAY'S END

I prefer to end each day the same,
On my porch to view the setting sun.
And just look out over this old claim,
Like a tired dog, whose day is done.

It's how I tally loss or gain,
Of each day that I've been blessed.
Far removed from all the pain,
Of a world by greed possessed.

No sabers rattled here tonight,
No threats lay wait to mar my peace.
Reflections in the waning light,
Breeze so soft as virgin fleece.

These pensive musings are my wage,
Accrued each day to my account;
They tame the beast, lay waste to rage,
No lies to sort and then discount.

On the air is stark distress,
It seeks me out, where I may hide.
To steal from me my happiness,
And fill me brim with foolish pride.

This hopelessness I cannot bear,
Aimless curs in hordes amass.
They charge headlong without a care,
Oblivious to all they pass.

I shield myself as best I can,
Lest recluse, might I soon turn.
On my porch, these woes I ban,
So little time, so much to learn.

Far from sirens wailing shrill,
Far over head I curse a plane.
I thirst for peace, and drink my fill,
By myself, immune to pain.

DO YOU REMEMBER WHEN?

Do you remember when, old friend,
We toiled in forests deep and damp?
When danger lurked 'round every bend,
And we called home a logging camp.

Do you remember those long plank roads,
The days we used to log with teams?
And when we learned to move our logs,
With wire rope, and power from steam.

Can you still see the spars we topped,
And hear the blocks hum way up high?
We hopped up on the stumps we chopped,
And watched the lines dance in the sky.

And who could forget those misery whips,
So truly named, and rightfully so.
We fell the spars for the sailing ships,
That took our wood where the four winds blow.

Can you recall those Saturday nights,
We got so hog jawed, we couldn't see;
And those bare knuckle bar room fights,
We stood back to back pard, you and me.

Now those new fangled Diesels roar,
Our logging camps, a relic of the past.
Machines make ease of what was our chore,
And the life we knew, now gone at last.

Will they remember us old friend,
When we have gone on to our grave?
Will they say, "do you remember them,
Those timber tramps, and all they gave?"

GLOSSARY

BALDWIN: Brand name of and old time steam engine used to transport log trains from the woods to the mills.

BARBER CHAIR: When a tree slabs off and splits up the middle, with the main part falling to the ground, haphazardly, and the other part remaining on the stump, giving it the appearance of a barber's chair.

BELL: A heavy slotted part of the choker, which the nubbin fits in.

BOOM STICK: Very long, sound pieces used for making log rafts.

BRUSH: Slang term for the woods

BUCK: The sawing up off a tree into logs.

BUG: Talkie tooter, the device that signals the whistles that loggers communicate with.

BULL BUCK: The supervisor of the cutting, or felling crew.

BUTT CUT: The first, and biggest portion of a log being bucked into manageable lengths for yarding.

CAMP: Temporary home in the woods for the logging crews.

CAN TO CAN'T: Working your ass off.

CAT: Caterpillar tractor: i.e., a bulldozer.

CAULKS/CORKS: A logger's spiked or hobnailed boots.

CHASER: The man who runs the landing.

CHISEL BIT: Type of saw chain, preferred by timber fallers, for its fast cutting.

CHOKER: Length of wire rope with a nubbin on one end that fits into a slotted bell, which slides the length of the cable and cinches tight around the log.

CHOKER DOG: The choker setter

COLD DECK: A large deck of logs stored for later loading.

CRUMMY: A crew bus, loggers transportation to the job site and back.

CULL: Any thing not up to par, a lousy logger is called a cull.

DOG: A mechanical device for securing a drum; sharp points on the power head of a chain saw used for making the saw more stable during cutting.

DONKEY: A steam powered engine used long ago for the yarding and loading of logs.

DRUM: A large, geared, steel cylinder that wire rope is spooled on, attached to a power source and equipped with brakes used for yarding and loading.

DUFF: Layer of decomposed material lying on the forest floor.

ENGINE: Locomotive.

FACE: The front cut made in the felling of a tree.

FLY BLOWED: State of disrepair/drunk.

GUY LINE: Strong steel cables attached to the top of a tower or spar tree on one end and a stump on the other end, to stabilize it during logging operations.

GYPO: Small time logging outfit.

HANG UP: An obstacle to overcome in the logging operation.

HAULBACK: The line that returns the rigging back to the crew in the brush.

HAYWIRE: Small diameter cable used for pulling the larger lines in making your lay out.

HIGH BALL: To give it all you've got, to work very fast.

HIGH LEAD: Method of logging incorporating two drums and a spar or tower for lift.

HOG JAWED: Fouled to a stand still/Drunk.

HOIST: A set of yarding drums.

HOOK TENDER: The supervisor of a logging crew.

JAKE BRAKE: Jacobs brake on a Diesel engine, an engine compression brake.

KIBOSH: To upset things, a disaster.

KICKER: A rigging trick used to kick a log around or over a hang up.

KONK: A defection in a tree.

LANDING: The central point of a logging operation, where the logs are yarded and stored for shipping to the mill.

LEANER: A tree leaning heavily to one side.

MACK: Brand of truck.

MARLIN SPIKE: Long tapered steel spike, used to separate strands in wire rope, to facilitate splicing.

MISERY WHIP: An old time logger's cross cut saw.

MOLLIE: A strand of cable used as a fastening device.

PETERBILT: A brand name of truck popular with log haulers.

PIKE POLE: Long pole with a hook and spike used by the old time river drivers.

RIGGING: The chokers and set of barrels, swivels, and drops that connect the main line and haul back to each other.

RIGGING SLINGER: The supervisor of the rigging crew.

SHEAVE: a large steel pulley device that directs the line towards the load.

SIDE ROD: Overseer, of logging operations.

SIWASH: A line run afoul of its normal lead, for a number of reasons.

SKIDDER: A large rubber tired, diesel powered tractor, equipped with grapples or a drum and arch. Used to move logs from the woods to the landing.

SLED: A large wooden platform constructed atop two large logs that the donkey and hoist are afixed to, it drags itself where ever it has to go.

SPAR TREE: A large, stout and tall tree rigged up with cables and blocks, with a donkey and hoist at its base.

SPRING BOARD: A long, wide plank with a steel tip that the logger notched into a tree to raise himself above the swell and defect of the tree base, in order to facilitate its felling.

TALKIE TOOTER: See; Bug

TIMBER TRAMP: A roustabout logger who makes the rounds of timber camps aka Gypo Gypsy.

TLINGKIT: A group of native Alaskans inhabiting the rain forests of the south east.

TOPPER: High climber, one who tops trees for use as a spar pole.

TOWER: A mobile yarding machine, often self propelled, mounted on rubber or tracks, equipped with a tall steel tower, to give the logger the advantage of lift in order to clear obstacles on the ground.

TWISTER: The connecting of two stumps, by means of a section of haywire, looped around and around and a chunk of wood serving as a windlass to cinch the whole works up tight, purpose being, to reinforce a guyline or tailholt.

TURN: Logger's vernacular for a group or bunch of logs being moved.

WANNABEE: A near do well logger/Cull.

WICKERVILLED: All messed up/Drunk.

WIDOW MAKER: A disaster waiting to befall an unsuspecting logger, and make a widow of his wife.

LOGGER'S LAMENT

A logger's life is rife with strife, and sometimes it's too much to take,
When life and death, a man's last breath, lay in wake of an honest mistake.
Sometimes he can't deal with the way folks feel, looked down upon, spat at, and scorned.
He feels defeated, let down and cheated, treated like a devil, evil and horned.
Tamers of the wilds, trail blazers, builders of our nation strong and great,
For all that he's given for the sweet life we're livin', so few could care less of his fate.

For additional copies and recitals please contact:

Michael J. Barker
Dunlogin, Inc.
86489 Lorane Hwy.
Eugene, OR 97405

541-343-6025 / 541-485-0528
Email: hoss75@msn.com